Building Hybrid Android Apps with Java and JavaScript

Nizamettin Gok and Nitin Khanna

O'REILLY®

Beijing · Cambridge · Farnham · Köln · Sebastopol · Tokyo

Building Hybrid Android Apps with Java and JavaScript

by Nizamettin Gok and Nitin Khanna

Printed in the United States of America.

Published by O'Reilly Media, Inc., 1005 Gravenstein Highway North, Sebastopol, CA 95472.

O'Reilly books may be purchased for educational, business, or sales promotional use. Online editions are also available for most titles (*http://my.safaribooksonline.com*). For more information, contact our corporate/institutional sales department: 800-998-9938 or *corporate@oreilly.com*.

Editors: Simon St. Laurent and Meghan Blanchette	**Cover Designer:** Randy Comer
Production Editor: Melanie Yarbrough	**Interior Designer:** David Futato
Proofreader: Linley Dolby	**Illustrator:** Rebecca Demarest

July 2013:   First Edition

Revision History for the First Edition:

2013-07-19:   First release

See *http://oreilly.com/catalog/errata.csp?isbn=9781449361914* for release details.

ISBN: 978-1-449-36191-4

[LSI]

I would like to dedicate this publication to my sons, Akira and Hiroki, and my wife, Yukiyo, for their support. I wouldn't be able to complete this without all of you.

— Nizamettin Gok

I would like to dedicate this book to my wife and parents; without their support, this book would not have been possible.

— Nitin Khanna

Table of Contents

Preface

This book is intended for an audience interested in building powerful HTML applications by bridging the gap between JavaScript and the device's native APIs. This book lays down a solid foundation for the architectural aspects of hybrid applications on Android, covering internals of WebKit and Android as needed. As part of this book, we have not only introduced some of the key web technologies used for building hybrid applications, but we have also focused on how they can be integrated into the Android build system. We will also be discussing some important aspects of hybrid applications from a security perspective.

To tie it all together, we are also introducing the Karura Framework. The purpose of this framework is two pronged. First, we want to simplify the overall process of integrating native components in hybrid applications. Second, we want to present a lean framework that is easy to read and write for. The framework itself is plug-in–based and can be extended and cut down based on the requirements of individual applications. We have released the framework under a dual license scheme. You can easily import Karura Framework into your project using Eclipse or the command line and start developing for it.

To reiterate, this book has been written with the purpose of allowing our readers to understand the following:

- What is a hybrid application?
- What goes under the hood in Android in the case of hybrid applications?
- What does the architecture of a hybrid application look like?
- What are some key tools and technologies for building next generation hybrid apps?
- What are the security considerations for hybrid applications?
- How do I publish an application in Google Play and Amazon App Store?

Conventions Used in This Book

The following typographical conventions are used in this book:

Italic
> Indicates new terms, URLs, email addresses, filenames, and file extensions.

`Constant width`
> Used for program listings, as well as within paragraphs to refer to program elements such as variable or function names, databases, data types, environment variables, statements, and keywords.

`Constant width bold`
> Shows commands or other text that should be typed literally by the user.

`Constant width italic`
> Shows text that should be replaced with user-supplied values or by values determined by context.

 This icon signifies a tip, suggestion, or general note.

 This icon indicates a warning or caution.

Using Code Examples

This book's accompanying files, libraries, and required frameworks (such as Karura) are hosted on GitHub. You can view them online or download them from *http://github.com/karuradev*.

We will continue to maintain the Karura Framework and will provide various examples of Hybrid Apps on GitHub as well. Should you have any questions or inquires about Karura Framework, please contact us at *karuradev@gmail.com*.

This book is here to help you get your job done. In general, if this book includes code examples, you may use the code in this book in your programs and documentation. You do not need to contact us for permission unless you're reproducing a significant portion of the code. For example, writing a program that uses several chunks of code from this book does not require permission. Selling or distributing a CD-ROM of examples from O'Reilly books does require permission. Answering a question by citing this book and quoting example code does not require permission. Incorporating a significant amount of example code from this book into your product's documentation does require permission.

We appreciate, but do not require, attribution. An attribution usually includes the title, author, publisher, and ISBN. For example: "*Building Hybrid Android Apps with Java and JavaScript* by Nizamettin Gok and Nitin Khanna (O'Reilly). Copyright 2013 Nizamettin Gok and Nitin Khanna, 978-1-449-36191-4."

If you feel your use of code examples falls outside fair use or the permission given above, feel free to contact us at *permissions@oreilly.com*.

Safari® Books Online

Safari Books Online is an on-demand digital library that delivers expert content in both book and video form from the world's leading authors in technology and business.

Technology professionals, software developers, web designers, and business and creative professionals use Safari Books Online as their primary resource for research, problem solving, learning, and certification training.

Safari Books Online offers a range of product mixes and pricing programs for organizations, government agencies, and individuals. Subscribers have access to thousands of books, training videos, and prepublication manuscripts in one fully searchable database from publishers like O'Reilly Media, Prentice Hall Professional, Addison-Wesley Professional, Microsoft Press, Sams, Que, Peachpit Press, Focal Press, Cisco Press, John Wiley & Sons, Syngress, Morgan Kaufmann, IBM Redbooks, Packt, Adobe Press, FT Press, Apress, Manning, New Riders, McGraw-Hill, Jones & Bartlett, Course Technology, and dozens more. For more information about Safari Books Online, please visit us online.

How to Contact Us

Please address comments and questions concerning this book to the publisher:

O'Reilly Media, Inc.
1005 Gravenstein Highway North
Sebastopol, CA 95472
800-998-9938 (in the United States or Canada)
707-829-0515 (international or local)
707-829-0104 (fax)

We have a web page for this book, where we list errata, examples, and any additional information. You can access this page at *http://oreil.ly/hybrid-android-apps-java-javascript*.

To comment or ask technical questions about this book, send email to *bookques tions@oreilly.com*.

For more information about our books, courses, conferences, and news, see our website at *http://www.oreilly.com*.

Find us on Facebook: *http://facebook.com/oreilly*

Follow us on Twitter: *http://twitter.com/oreillymedia*

Watch us on YouTube: *http://www.youtube.com/oreillymedia*

Acknowledgments

Nizamettin Gok

I would like to thank my colleague Sriraman Krishnamoorthy for his valuable input in this book. He is an excellent architect in the mobile space. I also would like to thank the passionate and talented technical reviewer Mauvis Ledford who helped review and correct this book.

It has been an amazing journey for me to complete this book. During this journey, I quickly realized that writing a book is not only a way of teaching someone, but also learning the correctness of what I have learned. For this reason, it is my ultimate pleasure to give back to the developer community.

Nitin Khanna

We would like to thank Mavious Ledford for reviewing the book. We would also like to thank our families, without their support and patience this book would not have been possible.

About the Technical Reviewer

Mauvis Ledford is a full-stack developer, speaker, and technical lead specializing in front-end technologies (CSS3, JavaScript, and HTML5) and cloud computing. He has worked and consulted for start-ups and companies large and small from Disney Mobile to Skype. He currently runs his own software company Brainswap (*http://www.brains wap.me*) focused on productivity applications.

## CHAPTER 1

What Is Android?

Android is many things, and the answer depends on who you ask. While for some it is an operating system optimized for mobile devices, others talk of it as an open source middleware and an application framework that allows developers to build applications primarily using the Java programming language.

What is Android? As a software stack, Android is an operating system from Google. Android is free and open source. Android is based on a mobile-centric version of the Linux operation system, at its core. As an application framework, Android packs a comprehensive set of advanced features for developers to build applications with rich user experiences and complex logic. As a middleware, Android offers a number of libraries to help developers build their next big ideas with ease. The Android Software Development Kit from Google contains all necessary tools to allow developers to code, develop, and test their applications on Android devices.

Because Android is open, there are a number of off-standard distributions of Android from OEMs like Amazon, Samsung, Motorola, and HTC to name a few. These distributions of Android have been heavily customized to support device profiles or brand-specific user experiences. For good or bad, this has led to huge fragmentation among Android devices. Hence, if you ask the IT department of any organization, Android and devices running Android pose a huge challenge when trying to provide users with uniform access to enterprise assets.

Android has been quite popular since its launch, and the fact that it is open source and enjoys a low entry barrier has led to its usage on platforms beyond mobile devices, including music players, ebook readers, televisions, wearable gadgets such as Google Glass or Android Watches, and so on. Because Android development is based around use of Java as a primary development environment, a huge pool of open source/COTS libraries are available to help you accelerate your application development process. This has also led to a huge surge in the need for Android developers. In summary, it is a good platform to learn in the short and long run.

Android Applications

An Android application is a mobile application developed using the Android SDK and targeted toward devices running the Android operating system or runtime (in case of Blackberry devices).

So now that we have some idea about Android and the fact that we are all motivated to build our next killer application for Android, one obvious question looms: In what language should you develop your application? What technologies would you have to learn and master for you to realize your next big idea: Java or something else? Contrary to popular belief, Java is not the only language you can use to develop software for Android. There are a number of tools available today to develop Android apps in C/C++, Python, Ruby, and HTML/JavaScript.

In this book, we will focus on a special category of apps, known as the hybrid applications using a mix of native Java and HTML/JavaScript.

In the rest of this chapter, we will lay down the definition of a hybrid application, and discuss the key architecture and runtime. We will also discuss at a very high level the APIs available in Android that can be used for building these applications.

What Is a Hybrid Application?

"Hybrid" applications are a special category of web applications that extend the web-based application environment through their use of native platform APIs available on a given device. The hybrid application design pattern is equally applicable to both mobile and desktop environments. For the scope of this book, we will focus on hybrid applications targeted toward the Android platform, however, most of the design patterns are also applicable to other platforms, including iOS and Windows Phone.

Categories of Applications

In general, applications can be broadly classified into four distinct categories: native apps, generic mobile apps, dedicated web apps, and hybrid apps. Let's look at each of these categories.

Native apps are the most common applications that you can find in app stores (application marketplaces) today. Native applications are usually developed using higher level programming languages, such as Java for Android, Objective-C for iOS, or C# for Windows Phone. The native APIs are provided to the developer as part of the platform SDK. The platform APIs are usually designed to provide native apps optimal access to hardware capabilities, such as the device's camera and Bluetooth stack. In addition, users may be able use these apps without an Internet connection. On the downside, since platform SDKs are based around different programming languages, developers need multiple implementations of the same application for them to be able to achieve any reasonable market reach. The development cycle is often tedious, costly, and involves a lot duplicate effort. Native apps are useful when performance optimization is very critical—for example, in simulations and high-end interactive graphics. Building native apps requires highly targeted platform-specific skills and a steeper learning curve, as developers have to deal with the nitty-gritty of the platform.

Generic mobile web apps are websites designed for web-enabled mobile phones. They usually look alike on all platforms and do not leverage platform APIs to customize the user experience for users. Visit Wikipedia mobile app (*http://goo.gl/AZ5t3*) for this example.

Dedicated web apps are web applications that have been tailored for a specific platform like Android, iOS, or Blackberry. A good example for this is LinkedIn web app (*http://goo.gl/j3HzI*).

Mobile web apps can be built using common server-side technologies such as NodeJS, PHP, and Ruby on Rails. Access to the app is usually gained by typing the URL address in the mobile browser. The assets and resources, including but not restricted to images, audio, video, CSS, and so on, for these apps reside on the web server. One potential downside of this approach is that downloading these assets onto the device may not only increase the cost associated with data usage but may also affect user experience due to latencies involved in such networks.

 HTML5 does offer an application cache mechanism that allows apps to cache the assets to device storage for the future use.

Hybrid apps, like native apps, run within a native process environment on the device. These apps typically wrap the HTML content within a web browser control in full screen mode, without a visible address bar or other browser chrome controls. Hybrid apps leverage the device's browser engine (the most common being WebKit) to render web content and process JavaScript code. Hybrid apps use a web-to-native abstraction layer (also known as bridge layer) that allows JavaScript to access many device-specific capabilities and native APIs that are not generally accessible from the mobile web browser alone.

Key Characteristics of Hybrid Apps

Unlike web applications or mobile websites, which the user can access by browsing to the URL, hybrid apps are typically installed through an app store and are available through the platform application launcher. This means users have to follow the same procedure to install hybrid application, as they would have for native applications. The platform will ask users to grant device access permission upon installation.

 At this point, we would like to cite a clear differentiation between a category of apps that we refer to as bookmark web apps, which are like hybrid apps in the sense that they are also downloaded from an app store, but are distinct in the sense that these apps are nothing more than a redirector or a shortcut for a website on the device. These apps usually terminate upon launching a browser session that redirects the user to the website for which this app was created.

Hybrid apps play a critical role in bridging the gap between the capabilities of the web browser and the that of the device, allowing developers to build applications that can benefit from the best of both worlds.

Hybrid apps are primarily written using a combination of HTML5, CSS, JavaScript, and platform-specific SDKs, such as Java for Android, Objective-C for iOS, or C# for Windows Phone.

A hybrid app package generally includes a bundled copy of all necessary web resources (i.e., HTML, JavaScript, CSS, and images) so that the app instantly loads like a native app, without waiting for a web server to deliver everything. Depending upon the complexity and size of the resources, some variants of hybrid apps may download device-specific content upon first launch. This allows developers to customize the application user experience on a per-device basis.

With the advancement in mobile operating systems and JavaScript processing engines, a hybrid app running on reasonably modern mobile devices can deliver highly efficient user experiences using bare HTML, CSS, and JavaScript for the UI layer instead of the devices' native platform programming language.

The hybrid approach provides developers with multiple advantages:

- Developers can update/rollback content and/or the application itself without requiring users to upgrade their application via a native app store. This is a huge advantage for content-oriented mobile apps.

- Developers can target generic UIs across multiple platforms, concentrating on the business logic and not the intricacies of each individual platforms' UI SDK. This is a huge win because in our experience, this saves developers close to 50% of development time through the lifetime of an application.

There is a lot value in developing platform-specific UIs, and you may eventually want to do it once your application usage crosses a certain threshold. Having said that, it should be relatively straightforward in the case of hybrid applications using CSS.

Why Developing Hybrid Apps Makes Sense

Hybrid apps have the unique ability of reaping all the benefits of traditional web applications without many of its limitations.

The benefits of hybrid apps compared to native include:

Faster time to market
> Building a hybrid application is typically faster and requires highly reusable standards skills. It does not involve a tedious learning curve when compared to native programming languages.

Inexpensive cross-platform development cycle
> Hybrid apps have cross-platform compatibility, reducing the footprint of native code needed, resulting in more reusable HTML5, CSS, and JavaScript that can be shared and deployed across platforms with minimal adjustment. This is primarily because WebKit is the platform of choice across all major mobile phone OSes today. Cross-platform development cycles also help keep the cost associated with development and testing under control. The reusability of HTML code allows developers to achieve a "develop once, deploy many" architecture. Native apps on the other hand would require developers to perform full-feature test rounds for platforms on which the application is being developed.

Abundant human resources
> Hybrid apps are built with web technologies, which means that there are many web developers who have the base skill set to build mobile apps.

Cost of maintenance
> Maintenance costs are usually lower because one does not need to rewrite (port) all application code to the native language of each device platform. Further, since the skill set to develop hybrid apps is readily available, scaling of a development team is also a nonissue.

Approval process
> Most of the app stores do have an approval process for which each app has to qualify before it can be made available through the sales channels of that app store. Because hybrid apps can be updated outside the bounds of an app store, you can typically get away with one submission to the app store. Once you are approved, you can push subsequent updates independently through your server if you like. A key point

to note however, is that a fresh submission of the application would be required every time you make changes in the native code associated with the hybrid app.

Hybrid apps are the future

Looking toward the future and upcoming advancements in mobile OS technologies, one can easily argue that hybrid apps are the future of development. Windows Phone 8, Google announcements to eventually merge Chromium OS and Android, Tizen OS, and Firefox all hint toward a hybrid future, not too far away, and hence, building and deploying hybrid apps is strategically a right thing to do.

The benefits of the hybrid apps compared to mobile web include:

Access to device capabilities

As mentioned in the introduction paragraph, hybrid apps offer the unique opportunity to reap all the benefits of traditional web applications without many of their limitations. Hybrid apps can extend the JavaScript environment to access the native APIs and capabilities of the platform that are not available through the generic web browser environment otherwise, for example, true offline storage, as well as access to contacts and other media on the device.

Unavailable new platform features

Hybrid apps can take advantage of the new features that are available in the new SDKs. However, you will have to develop and expose that native layer using plugins or a framework, which is usually the boilerplate code in most cases.

Distribution through app stores

Hybrid apps are distributed through app stores just as native apps are. You discover, download, and install them, as you would a native application. Therefore as a developer, you can leverage an existing well-established channel for content, app discovery, and monetization.

Offline access and execution

Hybrid apps, like native apps, can be run locally on the device when the device is offline—i.e., it is not connected to any network.

The possible drawbacks of hybrid apps as compared to native apps include:

Performance

You may experience potential performance issues because JavaScript is fundamentally single-threaded, which means that only one operation can be performed at a time. However, if done right, you can come up with a solution wherein you can offload background tasks to a native thread, which would execute in parallel while your app is busy performing UI operations. The native thread would then notify the JavaScript of the events and task completions/failures.

Differences in cross-platforms

WebKit is not equally maintained in all mobile platforms, which means that there might be indistinct differences between renderings and platform-specific features to watch out for, though one could arguably say it is a better scenario than rewriting all code from scratch. Further, this is such a well-understood topic that often you would find material describing ways to identify and mitigate these UI experience risks.

Unavailable advanced features

There might be advanced features that cannot always be easily implemented on the hybrid layer—for example, OpenGL-based rendering—however, the set of features is rapidly shrinking with companies like Microsoft, Google, and Mozilla introducing a bunch of new standards aimed at bridging this gap.

Inconsistent user interfaces

Platform-specific UIs' look and feel might be seriously difficult to mimic using HTML, CSS, and JavaScript.

The possible drawbacks to the hybrid apps compared to mobile web include:

Not accessible via website

A user is required to find your application in a native app store and cannot access it via a traditional web browser unless you've made one available.

 We believe that each of the solution strategies discussed in this chapter have both advantages and disadvantages respectively. Choosing the right technology for building a mobile app can be challenging. One should consider the implementation choices within the purview of the targeted mobile ecosystem and the application specifications and complexity.

Hybrid Application Architecture

Hybrid application architecture, shown in Figure 1-1, is a very high level view and will be described in a more detail later in this book. In addition, we will be covering a new hybrid application framework, which we have developed to substantiate your understanding of the concepts described in this book.

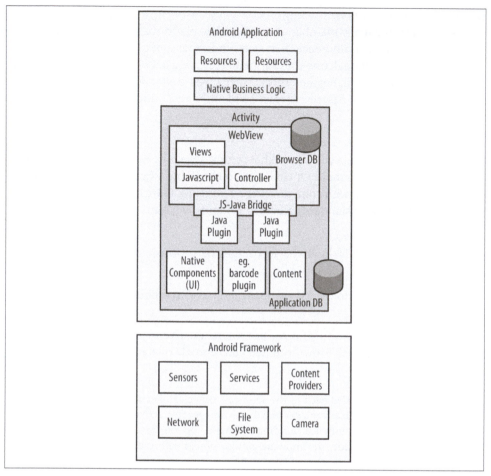

Figure 1-1. Hybrid application architecture

Key highlights of the architecture include:

- Application UI and business logic reside within a context of a headless web browser that is fully contained within your application.
- For features that are available within the web browser, the user interacts with the browser and the browser interacts with the native platform environment.
- Resources and assets are available locally or can be downloaded from the Web.
- For the platform features that are not natively available to apps through the standard JavaScript environment; custom extensions and plug-ins can be developed. These plug-ins act as a bridge, if you will, diminishing the gaps between the native and web environments.

In Chapters 5 and 6, we will address this topic in more detail.

How Do Hybrid Apps Work on the Android Platform?

Android's implementation of a WebBrowser Control is called a WebView. WebView uses the open source WebKit rendering engine to display and execute web content. The native Java APIs feature a number of convenience functions that can allow developers to take control of the user experience from native code. For example, they allow developers to navigate forward and backward through a history, zoom in and out, perform text searches, and more.

One of the functions exposed as part of the native WebView API is `WebView.addJavas criptInterface(Object object, String name)`. This method injects the supplied Java object into the WebView. The injected Java object can be accessed via the JavaScript as a global variable with the same name supplied in the Java function. This bridge functionality opens a communication channel between the Java and JavaScript layers. Hybrid apps take advantage of this abstraction layer that exposes the device capabilities to the UI layer.

This underused and powerful technique can come in handy when building hybrid apps, and we will show you how to take advantage of this feature in later chapters.

While we are on this topic, it is important to understand that the WebView model for extending Java into JavaScript is sort of nonlinear in nature. While JavaScript can call Java methods directly, the reverse is not true—i.e., functional callbacks are not possible from Java to the JavaScript environment. For calling methods into JavaScript from Java, `WebView.loadData()` and `WebView.loadUrl()` methods can be used.

One of the reasons for this skewed architecture is to support the fact that JavaScript runs in a single-threaded environment. Direct callbacks into the JavaScript environment could expose the JavaScript engine to multiple threads, which would be quite difficult to manage. Hence, by following a model wherein the native environment requests the WebView to load a URL or data, whenever it wants to call a function into the JavaScript, we emulate a message queue dispatcher, wherein each request to load data or a URL dispatches a new request to be executed in the order it was received.

## CHAPTER 2

Setting Up Your Android Development Environment

Hybrid applications involve a number of complementary technologies that are not native to the Android development environment and SDK. In this chapter, we will introduce you to some of the key technologies that will play a crucial role in helping us build our first hybrid Android app.

Most of the concepts described in this chapter are utilitarian in nature. These concepts will be used throughout the remainder of the book, so please go over them in detail.

The topics in this chapter range from setting up your development environment to the use of the various HTML, CSS, and JavaScript tools needed for an efficient development workflow. We will also cover some key design and implementation strategies related to mobile web application development. In addition to this, we will showcase some utility scripts that augment the Android build system to simplify day-to-day tasks.

In this section, we will describe how to set up the development environment for your hybrid Android application. For the scope of this book, we will use Eclipse as our primary development environment. Eclipse is a popular open source IDE that supports multiple languages and an extensible plug-in based architecture. The Android tool chain available from Google features plug-ins that can be integrated into the Eclipse workspace to streamline your Android application development experience.

Eclipse is not required for Android development but is a handy tool with a lot of features, as we'll describe later.

For installation, we will use an OS X based workstation, but any Unix-based system should work similarly. If you are on a Windows platform, we recommend using Cygwin so that you have an Unix-like shell.

Details about setting up the development environment can be found at the Android developer website (*http://goo.gl/8yu4c*) along with many other online tutorials. Although there are many resources and tutorials available on this topic, we recommend *Android Apps with Eclipse* by Onur Cinar (Apress) for some nifty tips about Eclipse.

 As of this writing, Google has introduced a new IntelliJ IDEA based IDE and tools for Android development. This IDE is still in its early beta stage and not very stable. We will update the chapters of the book and provide supplementary material on the website for using Android Studio for hybrid application development. Android Studio can be downloaded from the Android Studio website (*http://goo.gl/yqtsC*).

Before anything else, you will need the Android SDK from Google's Android SDK website (*http://goo.gl/KWUzQ*). Download the latest Android SDK and unpack the ZIP file into a desired location.

Installing Eclipse on Mac OS X

Eclipse for Mac is available as a GZIP package. Once you download Eclipse, it will be available in your Downloads folder. Depending upon the version of OS X you are using, you may have to double-click on the downloaded file to extract Eclipse. On newer OS X versions, Eclipse might already be extracted in the Downloads folder.

Installing Android Development Tools

Android Development Tools (ADT) comprise a set of open source development tools, available from Google. ADT is packaged as a set of Eclipse plug-ins, which extend the capabilities of the development environment, allowing developers to do the following:

- Create new projects
- Visually design UI
- Debug and unit test applications
- Provide assisted code development

You can find more information about ADT at the Android ADT plug-in website (*http://goo.gl/nlm5x*).

To install the ADT plug-in, select the Help→Install New Software menu option in Eclipse. This will display the Install dialog. Click the Add button, which will open the Add Repository dialog. In the Name box, type **Google ADT**, and in the Location box, type the following URL **https://dl-ssl.google.com/android/eclipse/**, and click OK. The Add Repository dialog will now close, and you will be back to the Install dialog. Now select the Google ADT repository, and select Developer Tools to install the ADT plug-ins.

 As of this writing, Google has also released a new integrated version of Eclipse and Android Development Tools called the ADT Bundle. Details for ADT Bundle can be found at the Android ADT Bundle website (*http://goo.gl/qQh1W*). This bundle includes Eclipse, along with Android plug-ins and the SDK preconfigured for development.

Creating Your First Hybrid Android Project Using Eclipse IDE

To create a new Android project in Eclipse, go to File→New→Android Application Project. In the Project Creation form, the Application Name is the one that will appear in the Play Store, as well as in the Manage Applications (Apps) list. The Project Name is typically the same as the Application Name but should be a unique name within the Eclipse workspace. Finally, you need to choose a Package Name as a fully qualified unique identifier, which will stay the same during lifetime of your application. Even if you release newer versions of your app, the package name must be retained, as this is used by various app stores to identify your application.

The API levels should align with your application specs. You can define the Minimum Required SDK as you target the lowest API level that you would like to support. The lower API levels serve more devices but restrict your apps to fewer features. API 8 and later can cover up to 95% of devices in the Android market.

In the Compile With selection, you choose a target API to compile your code against. For the Theme, we ignore any other options but choose None, because we are not designing a native app, and we will override the look and feel of application with JavaScript anyway.

You can also choose the highest API level that your application can work with in the Target SDK selection, specifying the minimum supported SDK to the minimal version you wish to support. If you decide to use this strategy for API selection, you will have to diligently build a user experience wherein you gracefully notify the users about features not available on the older devices. Figure 2-1 illustrates the application creation process.

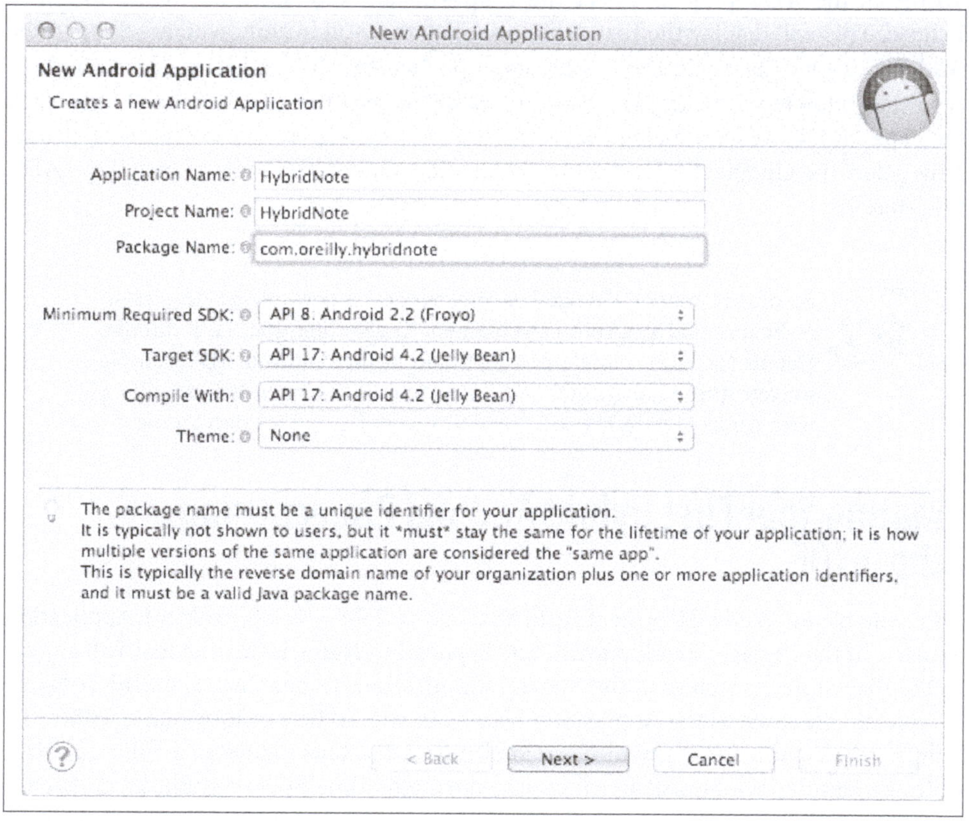

Figure 2-1. Creating a new Android Application Project using Eclipse

In the window shown in Figure 2-2, you define the location of your application in your workspace.

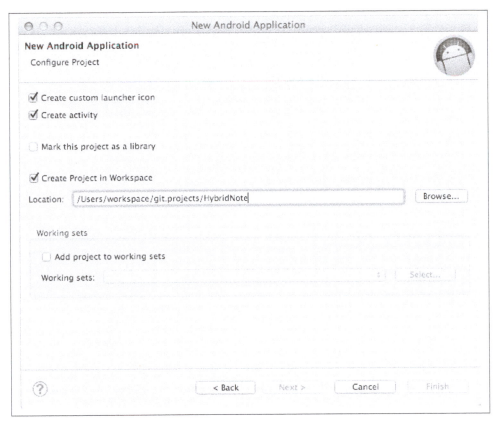

Figure 2-2. Defining your application workspace location

In the window shown in Figure 2-3, you provide a name for your main activity and its layout file. Typically, `MainActivity` is good enough.

Figure 2-3. Creating your main activity and its layout name

Android Development Using the Command Line

While Eclipse may be the platform of choice for development, we will be focusing more on a mix of Eclipse and command-line development. You can, however, integrate all these commands into Eclipse with ease, as described in *Ant: The Definitive Guide, Second Edition* (O'Reilly), for more details, visit the ANT with Eclipse instruction website (*http://goo.gl/hdsgM*).

Setting PATH Environment Variables

Once you have extracted the platform SDK on the filesystem, you need to set up your PATH[1] variables in the user profile for Mac OS X.

---

1. Before editing your profile file, you will actually see the list of paths that are already in your profile. Type **set** in the terminal to see the list of paths.

1. Open a terminal window.

2. Type **cd ~** to go to your home directory.

3. Type **touch .profile**[2] to create the hidden file named *.profile*, if one does not exist.

4. Type **open -e .profile** to open the file in the TextEdit application.

5. Then type **export PATH=${PATH}:${ANDROID_HOME}/tools:${ANDROID_HOME}/platform-tools**.

6. Save the file and exit TextEdit, and we are done!

The changes you made in your profile file may not be in effect yet on the current terminal, so you need to run source ~/.profile to enable the changes (you need only do this once for the current terminal). You can also just restart your terminal for a similar effect.

Here's an example of a *.profile* file:

```
# sample Android SDK tools and platform-tools paths for MAC
# export ANDROID_HOME=/Users/<username>/android-sdks
PATH=${PATH}:${ANDROID_HOME}/tools:${ANDROID_HOME}/platform-tools
```

What Is ADB (Android Debug Bridge)?

Mobile applications are often developed on a machine that is different from the device you finally deploy your solution on, and Android is no different. The machine on which you develop the solution is called a host, while the device for which the solution is intended is referred to as a target.

ADB is a handy tool that comes as part of the Android SDK, which allows you to interact with your connected Android devices or emulator (target) from the command line on the host. An Android device can be connected to the development host machine using either TCP or USB.

Basic ADB commands include:

adb devices
> Lists the devices (targets) currently associated with the host.

adb shell
> Opens a session to a basic shell running on the Android device.

---

2. *.profile* is a special file in your home directory, in the sense that the commands in the *$HOME/.profile* file are executed at login or open a new terminal session. These commands may be used to override the default environment behavior.

`adb install`

Installs an application (*.apk) file onto your device.

`adb uninstall`

Uninstalls an application from the device.

`adb logcat`

Streams the activity log from your device to the console.

`adb shell am start`

Sends an intent to the package manager component to be started. The intent may start an activity (application) or may just deliver the intent to an existing activity if it is already running.

`adb shell am instrument`

Starts an instrumentation. Typically, this target `<COMPONENT>` is in the form `<TEST_PACKAGE>/<RUNNER_CLASS>`.

`adb shell dumpsys <?>`

Dumps all available data about a given parameter. For example, you can get more information about the battery by typing the following command: **adb shell dump sys battery**. To get the list of services in Android from the command line, you can run `adb shell dumpsys | grep DUMP`. Once you get the result, you can then run each command individually.

`adb shell "am start -a android.intent.action.MAIN -n <packagename>/`
`<classname with packagename>"`

Launches the activity from command line. For example, you can try `adb shell "am start -a android.intent.action.MAIN -n com.example.package/com.exam ple.package.ExampleActivity"`.

Connecting an Android Device to the Development Host

Setting up a connection between an Android device and the host is very straightforward. If connecting via USB, all you need to do is connect the device and the development host via a USB cable. After this, you should be able to access the device using ADB or Eclipse.

 On Windows, you may have to install device-specific drivers before you can connect to a device. However, once the drivers are installed, the process is pretty much the same.

Connecting to an Android Device Over WiFi

ADB can connect to a device over WiFi as well. You can enable ADB over WiFi on the device by executing the following set of commands on the device.

```
adb shell
```

```
setprop service.adb.tcp.port 9999
```

```
stop adbd start adbd
```

On the development computer, you can connect to the device using the following command:

```
adb connect 192.168.1.1:9999
```

Make sure you replace 192.168.1.1 with the actual IP address associated with the Android device and 9999 with an available port on the device you wish to use for ADB.

The following command can be used to switch ADB back to the USB mode:

```
adb usb
```

Using Apache Ant to Automate Building Android Applications

To compile and package the application into what is known as an Android Package (APK) from the command line, we will use Apache Ant. Apache Ant is a command-line tool and a library (depending upon how you wish to use it) that can be used to automate the build process or tasks. Ant provides a number of prepackaged tasks to compile, assemble, and build Java applications. We chose Apache Ant as our command-line build tool because Google, along with Eclipse plug-ins, ships an Ant-based build system and associated tool chain.

Simply put, Ant is a tool that processes an XML-based scripting language to automate tasks. While you can provide any Ant-compliant XML file to Ant for execution, the default filename is *build.xml*. You can define all necessary build steps in this file. Each Ant XML file is described in terms of a project, target, or task.

 Google announced as part of the 2013 I/O conference that they will be migrating from an Ant-based build system to a Gradle (Groovy) based build system for Android. While the build system is still nascent, it holds promise. We will be releasing all our build scripts for Gradle eventually as the build system matures.

Here are some Ant terms with which you should be familiar:

Ant project

An Ant project is a group of targets, and tasks. A project is typically associated with a single build file.

Ant target

A series of Ant tasks to be executed in the order in which they are specified. An Ant target can depend upon a number of other Ant targets for completion, there by allowing us to build modular tasks.

Ant tasks

A unit of work that Ant can execute, such as compiling a source file, renaming files, and so on. As discussed earlier, there are number of tasks that come prepackaged with Ant. Users can develop their own tasks in Java or another scripting language as desired. As you delve deeper into the details of Ant, you'll realize the whole Ant task notion is very flexible and can be leveraged to perform very complex operations in a modular way.

To create a new Android project from the command line:

```
$ mkdir project_dir
$ cd project_dir
$ android create project -n HelloWorld -p ./ -t android-14
  -k com.helloworld --activity MainActivity
# -p is the path where the project files are to be generated
# -n Specified the name of the Project
# -t The android SDK to be used for compilation
# -k package name for the generated project
# --activity Name of the generated Activity Class
```

Here's the output of the preceding command:

```
Created directory
/Users/<username>/project_dir/src/com/helloworld Added file
./src/com/helloworld/MainActivity.java Created directory
/Users/<username>/project_dir/res Created directory
/Users/<username>/project_dir/bin Created directory
/Users/<username>/project_dir/libs Created directory
/Users/<username>/project_dir/res/values Added file
./res/values/strings.xml Created directory
/Users/<username>/project_dir/res/layout Added file
./res/layout/main.xml Created directory
/Users/<username>/project_dir/res/drawable-xhdpi Created directory
/Users/<username>/project_dir/res/drawable-hdpi Created directory
/Users/<username>/project_dir/res/drawable-mdpi Created directory
/Users/<username>/project_dir/res/drawable-ldpi Added file
./AndroidManifest.xml Added file ./build.xml Added file
./proguard-project.txt
```

You'll notice that upon execution, a number of files—including *build.xml*—will be generated by the Android tool. We will look at some of these files in this chapter. Let's look at *build.xml* for now.

```xml
<?xml version="1.0" encoding="UTF-8"?>
<project name="HelloWorld" default="help">
        <property file="local.properties" />
        <property file="ant.properties" />
        <property environment="env" />
        <condition property="sdk.dir" value="${env.ANDROID_HOME}">
                <isset property="env.ANDROID_HOME" />
        </condition>
        <loadproperties srcFile="project.properties" />
         <fail message="sdk.dir is missing. Make sure to generate local.proper-
ties using 'android update project' or to inject it through the ANDROID_HOME'"
unless="sdk.dir"/>
        <import file="custom_rules.xml" optional="true" />
        <import file="${sdk.dir}/tools/ant/build.xml" />
</project>
```

To create the Ant build system for an existing project created using Eclipse, run the following:

```
$ cd project_dir $ android update project -p .
# -p is the path
```

Executing this command generates a *build.xml* quite similar to the one just shown. The only difference being that, in this case, it will be able to retrieve Android target information and project details from the *AndroidManifest.xml* file in the current project folder.

Once you create the Ant build files in your project, type **ant help** on command line to see the available list of targets. (For Ant newbies, we are launching Ant and asking it to execute tasks associated with the help target.)

Now that we have a basic understanding of how Ant works, let's address the functionality of some common build targets you will be using through your development.

```
# cleans up the compiled files and generated resources
ant clean

# compile and package a debug version of the app
ant debug

# builds the debug version and installs it on the device or the
# emulator. Another interesting aspect to observe is that you are chaining
# multiple targets in the order they were mentioned on the command line
ant debug install

# builds release version
ant release
```

If you want to release your Android application to Google Play or any other app store, you need to self-sign your application with a certificate. Details about creating a self-sign certificate can be found at the Android application signing instruction website (*http://goo.gl/QD4RT*).

In general, you will execute the following command to generate a signing key:

```
keytool -genkey -v -keystore project_release.keystore -alias \
   project -keyalg RSA -keysize 2048 -validity 10000
```

After running this command, the key tool will prompt you for a password and a number of distinguished data fields to identify your key and the keystore. It then generates the keystore as a file called *project_release.keystore* in the current directory. The key store and key are protected by the passwords you entered. The keystore contains a single key, valid for 10,000 days. After having created a valid key store, you will have to inform the Android build system about the keystore to be used for your project. Do that by creating an *ant.properties* file in your project's base directory (in the same directory as *build.xml*). In this file, you need to specify the paths to the signing key and the alias.

```
# sample ant.properties file
# Relative path to the keystore
key.store=project_release.keystore

# The alias for the
key.alias=project

# The password which you supplied while creating the alias for the
key.alias.password=MyPassword

# Password for the key
key.store.password=MyPassword
```

Signing an application in Android associates it with a developer, which can then be used to ascertain valid updates and remove applications from the app store.

Understanding the Android Build Process

The build process is almost similar for Eclipse and command-line builds. Unless you are customizing the build process, they are one and the same. The Android build system compiles your source code along with resources, then packages them into a ZIP-compatible archive format. The build process on Android is composed of multiple stages. Let's look at these stages.

Resource Precompilation

The first step of the Android build system deals with autogeneration of an *R.java* file using the apt tool. This file is placed inside the *gen* folder, and contains constants for all resources in your project. The constants are used by developers to refer to resources inside the packaged application.

Here is a sample *R.java*, which was generated for the *hello world* project:

```
/* AUTO-GENERATED FILE.  DO NOT MODIFY.
 *
 * This class was automatically generated by the
 * aapt tool from the resource data it found.  It
 * should not be modified by hand. */

package com.helloworld;

public final class R {
        public static final class attr { }
        public static final class drawable {
                public static final int ic_launcher=0x7f020000;
        }
        public static final class layout {
                public static final int main=0x7f030000;
        }
        public static final class string {
                public static final int app_name=0x7f040000;
        }
}
```

Service Interface Precompilation

The second build step deals with autogeneration of Java code corresponding to the *service interfaces* declared in your project. Service interfaces are *aidl* files, which describe a service interface. In this step, the `aidl` tool looks at these files and generates the accompanying Java code. We will not look into `aidl` and service interfaces in this book; this topic has just been mentioned for completeness purposes. If you're interested in more details on this topic, you can visit the Android AIDL website (*http://goo.gl/8kSwI*).

Java Compilation

After the code autogeneration phase is complete, the actual Java source code and the autogenerated code is compiled to produce Java byte code. During the compilation process, the Android build system automatically adds the following files to your classpath (*.classpath*):

android.jar
> This file includes all android public APIs, stubs specific to the target platform for your application.

libs/.jar*
> Library jars you may have included in your project. These jars are located within the *libs* subdirectory.

DEX Generation

The output of the previous stage is a JAR file, which then needs to be converted into the DEX file format. DEX is the format supported by the Android or Dalvik virtual machine. In this step, the Android build system uses the dx tool to convert your application JAR and all other exported JARs into a single *dex* file.

Resource Packaging

Now resources are packaged into a partial ZIP file using the apt tool. While strings are placed in *resources.arsc*, the icons and other images are optimized and stored in this file preserving their relative directory structure in the resource folder.

Creation of the APK File

Next, the apk builder tool combines the resources and the *dex* file to create an application package for your application inside the *bin* folder. The apk builder includes the following components in the APK file.

- The Dalvik executable file *bin/classes.dex*

- Non Java resources in *src* folder

- Any native code, aka shared objects included in you project

- The partial resource package generated in the previous step along with the *resources.arsc* file

Once the package *apk* file has been created, it is signed using the debug or release key, depending on whether you are compiling a debug or a release build, respectively. The Android build system generates the debug key store automatically for your development purposes, which is located in the *$HOME/.android* folder.

Alignment

The final step of the build process deals with aligning the signed *apk* file to the 4 byte boundary. This is done using the **zipalign** tool. This step is primarily an optimization performed by the Android build system to allow the virtual machine to better memory map the resources at runtime.

Once the *apk* file has been aligned, it can then be installed on the Android device or an emulator.

CSS Preprocessors

CSS preprocessors take the CSS representational code written in a specific language to compile and convert it into the normal CSS format. Although CSS is really simple to understand, it can become hard to manage in a large scale project. With the help of CSS processors, we can maintain our CSS code easier and faster.

For example, consider a scenario in which you wish to use a particular shade of blue for your app across all the CSS files. Now, let's assume you wish to experiment with some other color scheme and would like to see how your application looks in the new color model. Traditionally, you would perform a mass search and replace within the CSS files, replacing old color values with new ones. This old method is cumbersome at best, as this kind of mass replace is often error prone because reverting the changes back may affect the other values.

This is where the CSS preprocessors become a really handy tool for many developers and designers. As you will see later in the chapter, you can use one of the several available CSS preprocessors to represent you application CSS in a more structured way, leveraging the concepts of object-oriented programming. This way, instead of replacing each instance of color or CSS attribute, you will focus on changing the base CSS classes with specific values. These classes are then inherited by others to create a more structured style representation for your app, thereby saving you time and preventing errors. CSS preprocessors are based around the DRY (Don't Repeat Yourself) principle. The syntaxes are much easier to read than normal CSS syntaxes because they employ more semantic markup.

There are many CSS preprocessors available for developers.

- SASS
- LESS
- Stylus
- Turbine
- Switch CSS
- CSS Cacheer
- CSS Preprocessor

We have chosen Syntactically Awesome Style Sheets (SASS) for building the CSS files for our application in this book. You can use any other available technologies; the principles involved are similar with only minor syntactical differences across these tools.

You can find a lot of invaluable information about SASS at the SASS website (*http://goo.gl/0Bw3U*).

Installing SASS

SASS was developed using Ruby and ships as a Ruby Gem. If you are using OS X, Ruby and Ruby Gems are preinstalled for you. To install SASS from the command line, use the following command:

```
$ gem install sass
```

For Windows, you will first install Ruby using an installer that can be found at the Ruby Installer website (*http://goo.gl/tXDmL*). Once Ruby is installed, you can in place SASS as previously described using the command line.

 If the command fails in Windows, please make sure you have Ruby and Ruby Gems in your path. Details on managing the path variables in Windows can be found at the Windows website (*http://goo.gl/ByoaB*) for managing environment variables.

Here is some sample SASS code:

```
/* -- application.scss -- */
$font_family: Arial, Helvetica;
$font_size: 1.6em;
$images_path: "../../img/";
$padding: 18px;
$height: 50%;
$header_color: #00FFDE;
```

 SASS files have .SCSS file extension. These are text files which can be created using any standard text editor.

Here is a simple usage of `$header_color` and `$font_size` in your SCSS file.

```
/* -- header.scss -- */
@import "application";
.main_header {
        color: $header_color;
        font-size: $font_size;
}
```

As you can see, SASS allows you to define variables, which can be used across multiple CSS classes, thereby avoiding the need for you to repeat yourself.

Use the following command to convert an *scss* file into a *css* file:

```
$ sass header.scss header.css
```

Once you run the command to convert the SASS file into normal CSS format, this is the output you will get (shown in Figure 2-4).

```
/* -- header.css -- */
.main_header {
        color: #00FFDE;
        font-size: 1.6em;
}
```

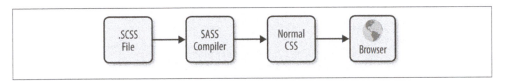

Figure 2-4. SASS conversion process flow

SASS has many nice features that will help you develop your CSS quickly with little hassle. For example, you can tell SASS to watch your SCSS files for any changes and convert them into CSS files on the fly:

```
# SASS will watch any changes in the +header.scss+ file
# and automatically update the +header.css+ with changes.
$ sass --watch header.scss:header.css

# SASS will watch any changes in the +sass_source+ directory
# and automatically update the files in the +stylesheet_output+
# directory with changes.
$ sass --watch sass_source:stylesheet_output
```

Integrating SASS into the Android Command-Line Build System

The following ANT `macrodef` defines a task that can be used to preprocess SCSS files to generate CSS files.

```
<!-- SASS - Converting SCSS files to CSS -->
<macrodef name="sass-css" description="SASS - Converting SCSS files to CSS">
        <attribute name="include-path"/>
        <attribute name="src-sass-file"/>
        <attribute name="dst-css-file"/>
        <sequential>
                <exec executable="sass">
                        <arg value="-I@{include-path}" />
                        <arg value="@{src-sass-file}" />
```

```
                    <arg value="@{dst-css-file}" />
            </exec>
        </sequential>
    </macrodef>
```

 For this task to work correctly, make sure that SASS is properly installed and the executable is reachable through the user path. You can
also provide the complete path to the SASS executable if that is not
possible.

The previous Ant macro can be called from anywhere within Ant to convert an existing
SASS file to a CSS file. For example, in the hybrid application we will be building in this
book, we have used the macro in the following way:

```
<target name="sass-css">
    <sass-css
        include-path="src/hybrid/css/ldpi"
        src-sass-file="src/hybrid/css/import.scss"
        dst-css-file="assets/css/ldpi.css" />
    <sass-css
        include-path="src/hybrid/css/mdpi"
        src-sass-file="src/hybrid/css/import.scss"
        dst-css-file="assets/css/mdpi.css" />
    <sass-css
        include-path="src/hybrid/css/hdpi"
        src-sass-file="src/hybrid/css/import.scss"
        dst-css-file="assets/css/hdpi.css" />
    <sass-css
        include-path="src/hybrid/css/xhdpi"
        src-sass-file="src/hybrid/css/import.scss"
        dst-css-file="assets/css/xhdpi.css" />
</target>
```

As you can see, we are exporting the CSS for multiple resolutions. You can customize
this code fragment to suit your application requirements.

JSLint Framework and Strict Coding Conventions

JSLint is a tool that was originally developed by Douglas Crockford for validating Java-
Script coding conventions. Although JSLint is not a proof of a program's correctness, it
can help detect problems in your code before they slip into your production code. JSLint
is highly configurable and has many features that can help spot incorrect syntax, un-
defined variables and functions, missing semicolons, erroneous expression statements,
and many other pitfalls.

jslint4Java is a command-line wrapper for the tool that can be integrated into Ant as a task. We will be using this task to automatically check the integrity of our JavaScript project every time we compile the project.

```xml
<!-- JSLint - Syntax-checks JavaScript files -->
<property name="jslint.dir" value="${out.dir}/jslint" />

<property name="jslint.version" value="1.4.7" />

<target name="get-jslint"
        description="JSLint - Syntax-checks JavaScript
        files" if="jslint-not-found">

    <mkdir dir="${jslint.dir}" />

    <get dest="${jslint.dir}"
            skipexisting="true"
            src="http://repo2.maven.org/maven2/rhino/js/1.7R2/js-1.7R2.jar"
            verbose="true" />

    <get dest="${jslint.dir}"
            skipexisting="true"
            src="http://repo2.maven.org/maven2/com/googlecode/jslint4Java/
                jslint4Java/${jslint.version}/
                jslint4Java-${jslint.version}.jar"
            verbose="true" />

    <get dest="${jslint.dir}"
            skipexisting="true"
            src="http://repo2.maven.org/maven2/com/googlecode/jslint4Java/
                jslint4Java-ant/${jslint.version}/
                jslint4Java-ant-${jslint.version}.jar"
            verbose="true" />

</target>

<target name="run-jslint">

    <available file="${jslint.dir}/js-1.7R2.jar"
            property="js-1.7R2.present"/> <available
            file="${jslint.dir}/jslint4Java-${jslint.version}.jar"
            property="jslint4Java.present"/>

    <available
            file="${jslint.dir}/jslint4Java-ant-${jslint.version}.jar"
            property="jslint4Java-ant.present"/>

    <condition property="jslint-not-found">
            <not>
                    <and>
                            <isset property="${js-1.7R2.present}"/>
                            <isset property="${jslint4Java.present}"/>
```

```
                              <isset property="${jslint4Java-ant.present}"/>
                    </and>
            </not>
      </condition>

      <antcall target="get-jslint"/>

      <taskdef name="jslint"
            classname="com.googlecode.jslint4Java.ant.JSLintTask" >

            <classpath>
                  <pathelement location="${jslint.dir}/js-1.7R2.jar" />
                  <pathelement
                        location="${jslint.dir}/
                              jslint4Java-${jslint.version}.jar" />
                  <pathelement
                        location="${jslint.dir}/
                                          jslint4Java-ant-$
{jslint.version}.jar" />
            </classpath>
      </taskdef>

      <jslint haltOnFailure="true" >
            <formatter type="plain" />
            <fileset
                  dir="${src.dir}/js"
                  excludes="vendor/**/*.js"
                  includes="**/*.js" />
      </jslint>
</target>
```

In this Ant task, if the `jslint4Java` for Ant is not available locally, we can download the specified version *jslint4Java-1.4.7.jar* file while building our project. Subsequently, we will use the existing version for all future builds. The latest version of `jslint4Java` can be downloaded from the jslint4java download website (*http://goo.gl/YMog8*).

Process HTML Templates

John Resig (creator of jQuery) is said to be the person who first popularized the concept of HTML templates within script tags. Visit the JQuery Micro-Templating website (*http://goo.gl/sddeF*) for more information. The idea is to preload the markup data and logic within a script tag with an invalid script type. The browser automatically ignores script tags with *invalid* types but we are free to access the content via JavaScript. This is a lot better than the older way of using hidden div tags because it is less memory intensive and more performant.

We leverage this concept and take it a step further. Basically, the idea is to build the user application using HTML templates, and then merge these templates into *index.html* during compilation.

Following is an example of what an HTML template looks like. Templates can not only contain regular markup but actual conditional logic to be used by template processors. The `type="text/x-tmpl"` makes this script invalid to the JavaScript interpreter. The purpose of this is that we want the WebView or browser to ignore the content within these tags and keep them nonrendered because we will be rendering these templates using JavaScript. All the placeholder variables in the template will be replaced with the real values using our JavaScript template engines. We will introduce more details about JavaScript templating techniques in later chapters.

We have used *Underscore.js* for the templating engine in our sample project.

```
<script id="tmpl_about_index" type="text/x-tmpl">
        <section class="content about">
                <div class="wrapper">
                        <span class="title">About Hybrid Note</span>
                        <span class="summary">Hybrid Note is a productivity app
for taking your notes...</span>
                        <span class="version">Version <%= data.app_version %></
span>
                        <span class="copyright">Copyright <%= data.current_year
%> Hybrid Note</span>
                </div>
        </section>
</script>
```

To facilitate the merging of HTML templates, we've built an Ant task to concatenate and append all our templates inside the *index.html* file.

```
<!-- Templates - Process HTML templates files -->
<macrodef name="templates"
        description="Templates - Process HTML templates files" >

        <sequential>
        <!-- merge all template files into templates.html -->
                <concat destfile="${out.dir}/templates.html" >

                        <fileset dir="${src.dir}/templates"
                                includes="**/*.tmpl" />
                </concat>

                <loadfile property="templates"
                        srcFile="${out.dir}/templates.html" />

                <copy file="${src.dir}/index.html"
                        overwrite="true"
                        todir="${assets.dir}" >

                        <filterset>
                                <filter token="templates"
                                value="${templates}" />
                        </filterset>
```

```
        </copy>
      </sequential>
    </macrodef>
```

Minifying CSS and JavaScript Files Using YUI Compressor

As you are developing for mobile phones and potentially would be downloading content over the Web, it is important to send as few bytes as possible of CSS and JavaScript over the network. Also keep in mind that it is not only the minimum number of bytes we should send, but the fact they should be sent across in a minimum number of requests. The minifiers are utilities that compress CSS, JavaScript, and HTML markup files, while still retaining the structure of code, thereby reducing the amount of data transmitted over the wire.

YUI Compressor is a Java-based, free, open source tool. It is one of the most popular JavaScript minifier tools, designed to be very safe and yield a better compression ratio. The YUI Compressor can also compress CSS files. With the help of YUI Compressor and Ant, we can consolidate our JavaScript and CSS files, then compress and combine them into a single minified version, one for CSS and one for JS, in order to obtain faster loading time and optimize overall performance.

```
<!-- tells Ant to refer to your environment vars -->
<property environment="env" />

<!-- defines location of YUI Compressor -->
<property name="lib.dir" value="${env.COMPRESSOR_HOME}" />

<!-- defines output directory -->
<property name="build.dir" value="build" />

<!-- output files, one for JS one for CSS -->
<property name="final_js" value="${basedir}/js/complete.js" />
<property name="final_css" value="${basedir}/css/complete.css" />

<!-- define nicknames for libraries -->
<property name="yui-compressor"
          location="${lib.dir}/yuicompressor-2.4.2.jar" />

<property name="yui-compressor-ant-task"
          location="${lib.dir}/yui-compressor-ant-task-0.5.jar" />

<!-- adds libraries to the classpath -->
<path id="yui.classpath">
  <pathelement location="${yui-compressor}" />
  <pathelement location="${yui-compressor-ant-task}" />
</path>

<!-- define tasks -->
<taskdef name="yui-compressor"
```

```
            classname="net.noha.tools.ant.yuicompressor.tasks.YuiCompressorTask">
        <classpath refid="yui.classpath" />
</taskdef>

<!-- targets -->
<target name="-concat">

    <!-- concatenates all compressed JS files into one -->
    <concat destfile="${final_js}" force="true" fixlastline="true">
        <fileset dir="${build.dir}" includes="**/*.js" />
        <fileset dir="${build.dir}" includes="**/widgets/*.js" />
    </concat>

    <!-- concatenates all compressed CSS files into one -->
    <concat destfile="${final_css}" force="true" fixlastline="true">
        <fileset dir="${build.dir}" includes="**/*.css" />
        <fileset dir="${build.dir}" includes="**/flexgrid/*.css" />
    </concat>

</target>

<target name="-minify">

    <!-- compresses each JavaScript and CSS file -->
    <!-- and saved as {original_name}-min.{extension} -->
    <yui-compressor
        warn="false"
        munge="true"
        preserveallsemicolons="false"
        fromdir="${basedir}"
        todir="${build.dir}"
    />

</target>

<!-- creates the temporary directory -->
<target name="-pre-minify">
    <mkdir dir="${build.dir}" />
</target>

<!-- deletes the temporary directory and all its contents -->
<target name="-post-minify">
    <delete dir="${build.dir}"/>
</target>

<target     name="min-web-assets"     depends="-pre-minify,-minify,-concat,-post-
minify" />
```

Using Safari and Chrome Browsers for Faster JavaScript Debugging and UI Changes

From time to time, you may want to open your HTML files in your browser in order to debug your JavaScript or try out different CSS values using Web Inspector in Safari or using Developer Tools in the Chrome browser. Safari and Chrome are the best to use in these situations as they feature a profile of the WebKit that is also used across mobile devices. With the help of the following Ant task, we can launch your app's HTML file in the browser using the following Ant command.

```
$ ant open-browser

<!-- Safari - Opens the Safari browser with mockup data -->
<target name="open-browser" description="Opens the Safari browser with mockup
  data">
    <exec executable="open" >
        <arg value="-a" />
        <arg value="safari" />
    </exec>
</target>
```

The **kill-safari** shell script exits the Safari browser.

```
#!/bin/sh
PIDS=`ps ax | grep 'Safari' | grep -v grep | sort | \
 awk '{print $1}' | perl -ne 'chomp;print "$_ "'`
if [ "$PIDS" ]
  then kill $PIDS
fi
echo "waiting for runner to start"
sleep 3s
```

## CHAPTER 3

Android Fundamentals

In this chapter, we will introduce you to the basics of the Android application framework. You can skip to the next chapter, if you are already comfortable with Android.

Android Application Architecture

An Android application is an archive that includes a combination of compiled Android components, a manifest file, and a bunch of resources and assets. We will look at these in more detail in this chapter. The archive is a file with an APK (Android package) extension. To put it simply, an APK file is a fancy JAR file. More details on the APK file format can be found at the Wikipedia website (*http://goo.gl/HCjs4*) for APK definition.

Android application framework and middleware are highly componentized and very flexible for UX customizations on a per-application basis. Android is secure, in that applications run in their own address space and an isolated sandbox that has limited or no access to other applications' data.

Despite all the security features, the Android application framework has been written from the ground up to allow application components to cooperate with those declared in the same or other apps to deliver a rich experience. This functionality is quite unique to Android and has been one of key driving factors for its success among developers. This topic will be further detailed later.

Key Android Components

The following sections outline the components that are necessary to programming for Android.

Dalvik Virtual Machine (DVM)

Android applications run on a mobile optimized version of JVM developed by Google, known as Dalvik Virtual Machine (DVM), which gets its name from a town in Iceland. The DVM toolkit features a `dex compiler`, optimizer, and a runtime. DEX is an acronym for Dalvik executable. During compilation, `Dexer` or the `Dex` compiler takes the regular Java byte code and converts it into the `dex` format, which is then packaged as part of the APK. Once `dex` code has been generated for the application, a tool known as `dexopt` is used for verification of the `dex` code.

Dexpot does its verification by performing an abbreviated VM initialization. It then loads zero or more DEX files from the bootstrap classpath and sets about verifying and optimizing whatever it can from the target DEX. On completion, the process exits, freeing all resources. In addition to this, DVM may perform some additional optimizations at runtime the first time the DEX code is loaded. Almost all of these optimizations deal with intelligently replacing sections of code with either one of pre-computed output, inline expansion of functions, or optimizing call flows.

View

A *view* represents a basic building block for a user interface in Android. It is rectangular in shape and is responsible for visual representation and event handling.

Activity

An *activity* represents the visual screen of an android application with which users can interact. An activity controls a group of views and usually correspond to a single logical screen of the app. An activity in Android creates a window over which UI components can be placed. We will discuss activities in more detail in subsequent sections.

Fragment

A *fragment* is a component with which users can interact. Fragments are like activity in most cases, except an activity can contain multiple fragments. Fragments were originally introduced in HoneyComb to support larger activities that had multiple UI components and complex logic driving the life cycle and event handling for these components. Larger activities resulted from the availability of larger screens, wherein there was enough real estate for developers to build very complex user experiences. In essence, fragments give developers an opportunity to group their views into logical blocks that can then be managed by the activity as opposed to managing them all at one level.

While the original driving factor for fragments was to modularize the UI, Android took the concept a little further by allowing fragments to inherit a life cycle similar to that of an activity. It must however be noted that a fragment's life cycle is driven by the life cycle of the activity with which it is attached. Doing this allowed fragments to be self-contained blocks of code without much dependence on the activity. This architecture goes a long way, as it then allows developers to dynamically instantiate, dispatch, and combine these fragments with ease.

Because fragments can be dynamically instantiated, replaced, and combined within an activity, Android also features a transactional model for performing fragment operations. The transactional approach allows users to group a set of fragment operations before they are dispatched for execution.

You can find more details on fragments from the Android Fragment API website (*http://goo.gl/Ehqku*).

Intent

An *intent* represents a message, request, or notification sent from one Android component to another. The intent framework is one of the most important IPC mechanisms built into the platform. An intent can contain additional parameters to better qualify the message for the receiver.

Services

A *service* in Android is a task that does not have an associated UI and runs in the background. Services are usually deployed to perform long running operations. Like an activity, a service can be consumed by components in a different application.

Content Providers

Content providers are data management components for storing a structured set of data in Android, which allows totally unrelated applications to share data. One of the salient features of the content provider framework is that it exposes a very RESTish interface to access data from within the device. The structured data source and individual records can be addressed as URIs on which CRUD operations can be performed.

Content providers can also implement a protection model around data access, thereby preventing unauthorized applications from getting the data.

While developers can write their own content providers, Android comes with a rich set built in. Information about these can be found at the Android android.provider API website (*http://goo.gl/NpIVK*).

Broadcast Receiver

As discussed earlier, intents are heavily used in Android for interprocess communication. Intents can either be directed to specific components or can be broadcasted to every component in the device. Depending upon the nature of intent and whether it is broadcasted, it may be received by more than one component. Broadcast is a handy strategy often used by system components to broadcast system state. One of the key advantages of this strategy is that Android will instantiate a component in case it has expressed interest in a specific kind of intent but is not currently running.

A *broadcast receiver* is a application component that listens for incoming intents.

Security Model in Android

Android also implements an access control system, which restricts applications from consuming any APIs for which they have not been authorized. APIs are associated with privilege levels. Every application in Android declares a set of privileges it would like to gain access to. When an application is installed on an Android device, the application framework notifies the device user of the request privileges and their significance and asks for the user's consent. An application will only be installed once the user approves the privileges required by the app.

Applications that serve other components in the device can also declare privileges and hence control who can access them during normal course of operation.

The Android security model is based around the notion of secured installation philosophy. This means application privileges are not granted at runtime. Privileges are granted only once during installation.

Resources

Resources are supplemental assets needed for visual representation of the app. Styles, dimensions, strings, screen layouts, shapes, and images all can be collectively referred to as resources. The resources in an Android app are inside the *res* folder of your application. Resources play a very important role in the Android application architecture. The most important being that one can change the resources of the application, and hence the look and feel of the app, without changing the code. This strategy allows developers to separate UX from code. What makes resources special from the developer standpoint is that, except for a special category of resources—i.e., raw—Android interprets the resources for you and provides you with a number of convenient functions to pick the right set for your device and configuration. For example, instead of using string literals in the code, you would use an Android generated ID. This indirection allows Android to yield appropriate strings based on device language and locale, and allows you as a developer to specify different sets of strings outside the source code.

The syntax you use to allocate an ID to a resource in the XML file is called *resource-reference syntax*. This syntax is not limited to allocating just IDs: it is a way to identify any resource such as a string, a layout file, or an image.

How is this general-purpose means of locating a resource or referencing an existing resource tied to IDs? IDs are numbers that are tracked as resources much like strings. Imagine your project holding a bucket of numbers. You can take one of those numbers and allocate it to a control.

Let's first investigate this resource-reference structure a bit further. This resource reference has the following formal structure: - @[package:]type/name.

The type corresponds to one of the resource-type namespaces available in *R.java*, some of which follow:

- R.drawable
- R.id R.layout
- R.string
- R.attr
- R.plural
- R.array

If you recall the *R.java* file, discussed in Chapter 2, you'll notice that there is an entry corresponding to each resource. The generated IDs are integers. Most methods that take strings also take these resource identifiers as inputs. Android resolves those ints to strings where necessary depending upon the device configuration.

```
<?xml version="1.0" encoding="utf-8"?>
<resources>
    <string name="app_name">MainActivity</string>
</resources>

/* AUTO-GENERATED FILE.  DO NOT MODIFY.
 *
 * This class was automatically generated by the
 * aapt tool from the resource data it found.  It
 * should not be modified by hand.
 */

package com.helloworld;

public final class R {
    public static final class attr {
    }
    public static final class drawable {
        public static final int ic_launcher=0x7f020000;
    }
    public static final class layout {
        public static final int main=0x7f030000;
    }
    public static final class string {
```

```
        public static final int app_name=0x7f040000;
    }
}
```

String Resources

Android allows you to define strings in one or more XML resource files. These XML files containing string-resource definitions reside in the */res/values* subfolder. You can use any name for the file, however, usually developers and Android build systems use *strings.xml*. You can also split your strings across multiple files, and Android will handle them just fine.

Layout Resources

Android provides convenience methods to load a view from an XML file, which make up a *layout resource*. The XML file is quite similar to an HTML file in terms of describing the content and layout of a web page. Lets look at a sample XML layout resource file:

```
<?xml version="1.0" encoding="utf-8"?>
<LinearLayout xmlns:android="http://schemas.android.com/apk/res/android"
    android:orientation="vertical"
        android:layout_width="fill_parent"
        android:layout_height="fill_parent" >

    <Button android:id="@+id/format"
                android:layout_width="wrap_content"
                android:layout_height="wrap_content"
                android:text="@string/btn_name"
                android:onClick="doSomething" />
</LinearLayout>
```

Inside your activity, you can send a request to Android to load a view description from an XML file using the setContentView() method. This is one of the several available options for loading views in Android. The process of loading a view from an XML file is known as *inflation*. This pattern is used widely in Android, and hence, we will spend a bit more time on this topic.

When you send a request to Android to load a view from an XML file, Android internally creates each and every view in the order in which they are specified in the XML. All the properties defined for the view are passed to the constructor of the view by the Android framework. The views are expected to apply the properties to incorporate any user-specified customizations. The views are then woven with each other in order of view hierarchy. The code would look something like:

```
public class MyActivity extends Activity {
    protected void onCreate(Bundle savedInstance) {
        super.onCreate(savedInstance);

        final LinearLayout ll = new LinearLayout(this);
```

```
ll.setLayoutParams(LinearLayout.FILL_PARENT, LinearLayout.FILL_PARENT);

final Button button = new Button(this);
button.setId(R.id.format);
button.setText(R.id.btn_name);

ll.addSubView(button);

button.setOnClickListener(new View.OnClickListener() {
    public void onClick(View v) {
        doSomething(v);
    }
});

setContentView(ll);
    }
}
```

As you can easily imagine, this can get quite large and complex based on the complexity of the UI. Inflation process hides this complexity from you as a developer, letting you concentrate on business logic.

There are other types of resources, as noted previously. Discussing them is outside the scope of this chapter.

Compiled and Uncompiled Android Resources

While most of the Android resources get compiled into a more optimum binary format, raw resources are copied as-is to the device. One key advantage of compiled resource files is that they allow you to pick correct resources based on device language. However, there may be times when you do not want this to happen. For such files, you can place them inside the */res/raw/* directory instead, they don't get compiled into binary format. However, because it is a resource, Android generates an ID through *R.java*. The resource type for raw files is raw. Audio and video files fall into this category.

Assets

Android offers one more directory where you can keep files to be included in the package: */assets*. It's at the same level as */res*, meaning it's not part of the */res* subdirectories. The files in */assets* do not generate IDs in *R.java*; you must specify the file path to read them. The file path is a relative path starting at the */assets* folder.

Structure of an Android App

If you recall the directory structure for an Android project, it looks something like:

```
├── AndroidManifest.xml
├── ant.properties
├── bin
├── build.xml
├── libs
├── local.properties
├── proguard-project.txt
├── project.properties
├── res
│   ├── drawable-hdpi
│   │   └── ic_launcher.png
│   ├── drawable-ldpi
│   │   └── ic_launcher.png
│   ├── drawable-mdpi
│   │   └── ic_launcher.png
│   ├── drawable-xhdpi
│   │   └── ic_launcher.png
│   ├── layout
│   │   └── main.xml
│   └── values
│       └── strings.xml
└── src
    └── com
        └── helloworld
            └── MainActivity.java
```

Let's have a quick look at some of these:

AndroidManifest.xml
> Android Manifest file.

src
> All your Java source goes here, by default anyway.

gen
> This is where the autogenerated code will be placed.

bin
> This directory holds the temporary binary output and the application once it has been successfully compiled.

libs
> This directory holds any third-party JARs your application requires.

res
> Here is where we store our styles, view layouts, strings, and so on.

res/drawable{qualifier}
> This folder inside the *res* folder contains the graphics files. The qualifier allows Android to pick up files based on device capabilities; it is a predefined suffix that you can add after *drawable* to help Android will pick the right resources based on

the device. In the previous example, ldpi is low dpi, and for devices that have very low density screens, images will be picked up from here. More details on resource resolution can be found at the Android Supporting Multiple Screen website (*http://goo.gl/9smqL*).

res/layout{qualifier}
Screen layouts in Android are XML files. In these XML files, we can specify what widgets we would like to use and how to lay them out on the screen. These files are located in the layout folders.

res/values{qualifier}
XML files that store various string values (titles, labels, and so on).

build.xml and .properties
These files are used for the Ant-based command-line build system. Please refer to Chapter 2 for more details.

proguard-project.txt
Proguard is a Java library that can be used to minimize, optimize, and obfuscate Java code. It optimizes byte code and removes unused instructions, symbols, and classes. It can also obfuscate the code by renaming classes and fields to smaller names, which makes the source code harder to read. The command-line builds for Android can express proguard on your apps. However, it is not enabled by default. This file is a sample proguard config, which you can use as the starting point for your app.

 You can enable the proguard builds for you app, by setting the pro guard.config property in the Ant build file.

Application Manifest

If you recall the directory structure for an Android project, you will find one of the files is named *AndroidManifest.xml*. Every Android project must contain this file in the root folder of the application project. This file is read by Android while installing or launching the application to determine application-specific information. The *AndroidManifest.xml* file describes the Android application and everything it can do.

Meta information contained within *AndroidManifest.xml* accomplishes the following:

- Helps Android OS determine the effective permissions for the applications and implement access control for any unintentional access to the platform by the app. The permissions described in the *AndroidManifest.xml* file are presented to the user at the time of installation, and only when the user accepts to grant these privileges does Android allow the user to install the app on the device.

- Declares the minimum level of the Android API that the application requires.
- Lists the libraries that the application must be linked against.
- Describes the background services implemented in the app.
- Allows the application to register for system events automatically.
- Allows the application to register as a content handler for specific mime types and actions. Actions determine whether the user is viewing, creating, or editing content.
- Describes the various UI controllers (activities) that are the UI entry points for the application.
- Declares the device capabilities needed by the app to function properly. This information is also used by the app stores to filter apps for certain devices.
- Declares the UI themes to be used for the application.
- Declares a test instrumentation runner to declare the component that can be used for unit testing.

And many more, which might be outside the scope of this book. However, we encourage you to look at the Android AndroidManifest.xml File website (*http://goo.gl/7owkl*) for more comprehensive details on *AndroidManifest.xml* and how it is used in Android.

The alert given before installation, shown in Figure 3-1, informs users of the requirements of the application. The user can then approve the installation of the application and the usage of the declared privileges.

 Because the user will be expecting the application to access only the information that is relevant to the application, we advise developers to only declare and use functionalities that are essential for the usage of your application.

If an application tries to access resources that are outside the scope of the application, users have more hesitation about installing the application for fear of loss of privacy/personal data.

Let's examine some of the important information that is declared in the application manifest file.

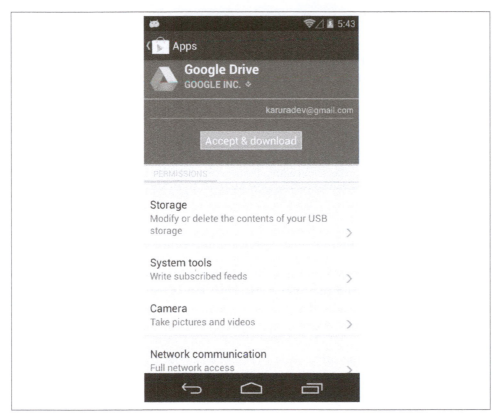

Figure 3-1. Install Privileges screen for a Google Play application

Application Package Name

The application package name is the name of the Java package that serves as the root package of the project. The package name is used as a unique application identifier by the Android OS.

The application package name can be declared in the Android manifest using the `pack age` attribute of the `manifest` tag.

An example of the package name declaration in the Android manifest can be as follows:

```
<manifest xmlns:android="http://schemas.android.com/apk/res/android"
        package="com.example.app"
        android:versionCode="1"
        android:versionName="1.0">
</manifest>
```

`manifest` is the root tag for the Android manifest file. In addition to the package attribute, it contains the `versionName` and `versionCode` attributes.

The versionName attribute describes the current version of the application in a human-readable form.

The versionCode attribute is a monotonically increasing positive number that is used by the Android OS to identify the latest version of the application. This value is used by the various app stores to generate analytics information for your app.

When debugging or collecting logs for an application, the package name can be used to identify the application and to filter logs corresponding to the application. Please refer the DDMS section of the Android developer website (*http://goo.gl/lIu1w*) for more tips on using DDMS.

Application

The class android.app.Application is the base implementation of a boilerplate application provided by the Android framework. This class serves as the *main* entry point to the application. Each Android application is required to declare one instance of this class. For most applications, android.app.Application should be sufficient, however, since this is the only pervasive class in the whole Android application, it is often used by developers to store application-wide accessible data. The Android OS will instantiate an object of this class whenever the application is launched. Android applications are special, and they stay in memory even when the user closed the UI screens.

Android continues to keep the application in memory until either the device is rebooted or it needs resources to be freed. Android does this to minimize application launch time. Because the application object remains in memory, it is important that we do not store references to huge data blocks in the application, or else Android will be forced to terminate and clean up the application when it goes into the background, preempting all optimization and resulting in a negative user experience.

The application tag in *AndroidManifest.xml* can be used to declare application-specific properties. Application-specific properties are described with the help of attributes defined as part of the application tag. Some commonly used attributes are:

name
Specifies the custom class to be used while launching the android application. This class must extend the android.app.Application class.

`icon`

Specifies the icon to be displayed in the Application Manager for this application.

`title`

Specifies the application title to be displayed by the Application Manager.

`description`

Any long descriptive text that you would like to supplement the title with for this application.

`hasCode`

Specifies whether this application has any code or not, noncode APKs are often used to deliver resource payloads on an Android device.

`hardwareAccelerated`

Specifies whether the application will use OpenGL-based hardware acceleration to render graphics on platforms that support this feature. In other words, enabling this flag will render smoother animations and graphics in your application. On older platforms, this attribute is ignored. This feature was enabled in Android version 3.0. Use of hardware-accelerated graphics is a CPU-intensive operation and can lead to higher battery use. Having said that, since not all 2D operations are optimized for hardware acceleration, Google recommends that you test your app to make sure it is stable when this feature flag is turned on.

`android:theme`

Android features a highly customizable user interface wherein you can customize different aspects of the UI by overriding platform style values using XML files. This tag allows developers to specify a style resource that describes the overall visual design for the application. Android will default all activities to the specified style for the given application.

Here's an example of the `application` tag in the Android manifest:

```
<application
        android:label="ExampleApp"
        android:icon="@drawable/example_icon"
        android:name=".ExampleApp">
</application>
```

The Java class name for various entities in the Application manifest can be specified as an absolute package path or, if prefixed with a period (.), will be appended to the package name. As in the previous example, the application class name can be specified as `.ExampleApp` or `com.example.app.ExampleApp`. They both refer to the same class path and can be referred to interchangeably in the manifest.

Make sure your package name does not include `google`, `android`, or `example` as the starting qualifier. Google filters out these apps and therefore, they cannot be published.

Activity

An *activity* is an application component associated with a screen with which users can interact to perform actions and receive feedback.

Android applications are based on the Model-View-Controller (MVC) architecture. MVC is a software pattern that calls for isolating data presentation from data and business logic. In MVC architecture, data is referred to as the model, presentation the view, and business logic is called the controller.

Activities correspond to the view controller in this architecture—i.e., they present a UI and implement the business logic to process events like touch and swipe.

An Android activity can receive user input if and only if it is running in the foreground. In Android, only one activity can be in the foreground at any given time. This is important to remember because although you may see multiple activities on the screen—for example, in the case of overlays—only the topmost can receive user events.

When the activity goes to the background, it is paused and when no longer visible, it is marked as a candidate for cleanup. Activities marked for cleanup may stay in memory for a long time. The actual time at which the activity is removed is determined by the OS. The application developer should not make any assumption about the time period that the activity is alive. Android will clean up these activities only when it is running low on memory.

The life cycle for an Android activity is modeled around a finite state machine, as shown in Figure 3-2.

While Android manages the life cycle of the activity, it notifies the developer of the transitions through callbacks. These callback methods are crucial to developing a strong and flexible application, as developers are expected to override these callbacks to inject their application-specific logic. An activity life cycle is also associated with other activities through the notion of a stack (also referred to as a task), through which a user can move backward. When a new activity is launched, it is pushed onto the back stack and is given user focus. When the user is done with the current activity and closes it, the topmost activity is popped from the back stack, and the previous activity is resumed.

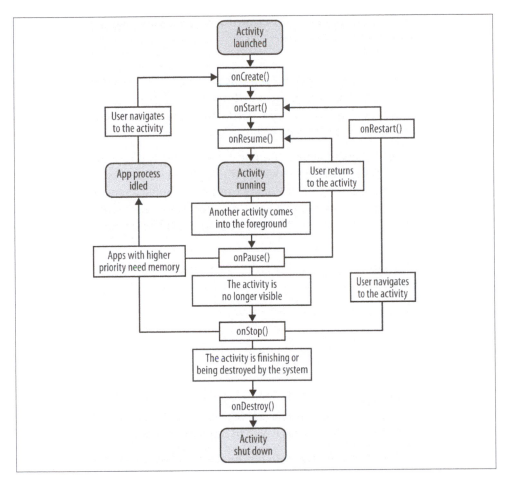

Figure 3-2. Activity life cycle (courtesy d.android.com)

From a life cycle standpoint, an activity can largely exist in one of three states:

Resumed
> An activity is considered to be resumed when it is in the foreground and has user focus. Some texts also refer to this state as the running state of the activity. In this state, the activity is associated with the Window Manager and retains the entire state of its member variables.

Paused
> An activity is said to be paused when it is still visible, but is behind another resumed activity. A paused activity is retained by the OS and kept in memory for the longest duration, unless the OS is running critically low on memory. Activities often enter a paused state when anther partially visible activity is displayed on top of an existing

activity. A paused activity is still associated with a window manager instance and can update the UI based on timer events.

Stopped

An activity is said to be stopped when it is completely obscured and sent to the background. It is no longer associated with the window manager. In this state, the activity may still be alive, however, it is marked as a candidate for cleanup for when the system is running low on memory.

Android allows developers to define multiple activities per application. Each of these activities can be launched from either within the application, as a result of user interaction with a different activity, or externally from other applications or the Android platform. There is no hard and fast rule as to when to define a new activity, however as a general rule, every logical screen of the application should be implemented as a separate activity.

The `activity` tag is used to declare an activity that has been implemented as part of the Android application.

An example of the `activity` tag is as follows:

```
<activity
        android:name=".ExampleActivity"
        android:label="Example">
</activity>
```

In the previous code snippet, an activity with class name `ExampleActivity` was declared, which is located at the application package level. Hence, if the application package was `com.example`, the fully qualified package path to the activity will be `.ExampleActivity`.

You can also specify a fully qualified path for the activity class in case the activity being declared is part of a different package than what has been declared in the application package identifier.

Some commonly used attributes for the `activity` meta tag are:

`name`

Specifies the name of the class that implements the activity. As described earlier, it can also be a fully qualified package path in case the activity is not defined in the application package path. This class must extend `android.app.Activity`, which is the base implementation of an activity in the Android platform.

`theme`

Android features a highly customizable user interface wherein you can customize different aspects of the UI by overriding platform style values using XML files. This tag allows developers to specify a style resource that describes the overall visual design for the activity. Android will apply the style automatically to the activity as it is created.

`configChanges`

Android manages configuration changes for you. Some of the scenarios treated as configuration changes in Android include rotating the device to change orientation, changing device, *Subscriber Identification Module card (SIM card)*, and so on. The default behavior of Android is to recreate the activity in this scenario. However, there may be times when you wish to manage configuration changes as part of your app. You can do this by specifying a list of configuration parameters in the value of this attribute. For all the parameters specified in this list, Android will pass on the information to the activity itself, by calling the `onConfigurationChanged()` method. You may override this method to perform application-specific logic.

An example for this tag is as follows:

```
android:configChanges = "orientation|keyboardHidden|keyboard|screenSize|locale"
```

In this sample, the activity will be notified of a configuration change every time the device orientation or language changes.

`exported`

Specifies whether this activity can be launched by external components within the device.

`hardwareAccelerated`

Specifies whether a hardware-accelerated OpenGL renderer is available for rendering the activity. The rendered graphics are smoother and optimized for visual performance. However, this may cause additional CPU consumption. If enabling this mode for you activity, you should thoroughly test your activity to make sure no side-effects are introduced, as not all 2D operations are perfectly supported by Android.

`icon`

An icon to be used for representing the activity.

`label`

A human-readable name for the activity. This is displayed to the user when the activity is being rendered on the screen.

`launchMode`

This flag informs Android as to how an activity must be launched, as in whether Android should recreate or reuse an existing activity upon receiving a request from the user. Available modes range from Android creating a new activity for each request or using a single instance of the activity for all requests.

`screenOrientation`

Specifies the supported screen orientations for the activity. Developers can use this attribute to switch the screen orientation to a specific mode.

windowSoftInputMode
> Specifies the nature of the soft keyboard and whether it is visible with respect to an activity.

Intents

Android, like many other mobile operating systems, is based on the notion of cooperative computing. One of the key aspects of this architectural approach is to allow software components within or across the app to work with each other in a complementary manner. An intent is an expression of request or a notification by a requesting component to the Android framework asking it to locate the best suitable component to service the request.

Intents play a critical role in Android's messaging framework and allow communication between, within, or across applications. Using the intent framework, the recipient of the message can be notified about something that has happened; for example, a system event or requesting the recipient to take some action such as showing the contact list.

An intent object can contain supplementary information necessary for the recipient application to decipher the message and take appropriate action.

Intents can either be broadcasted or targeted to a specific component within an application. Intents that are broadcasted are resolved by Android based on the match and the priority associated with the intent receivers. However, when targeted toward a specific component, Android simply passes on the message/notification to the component specified in the component object of the Intent.

Let's look at the structure of intent in a bit more detail:

action
> A string value specifying the request to be performed.

data
> Specifies the data on which this request has to be performed.

type
> Specifies the mime type of data being passed in the intent.

category
> Provides additional information about the action to be executed. In Android, you can have multiple components that can service the same action request, however, you may want to use these components in specific scenarios. category enables you to do just that. A category for an intent allows you to specify an additional attribute to your request, which can then be used by Android to dispatch the request to the right service module.

Intent Resolution

The process of delivering an intent to a target application is referred to as *intent resolution*. As described earlier, there two forms of intent you will end up using explicit and implicit.

The resolution in the case of explicit intent, is fairly straightforward, as you specify the component to which the concerned intent needs to be delivered. In Android, you can specify this intent by using the `setComponent(ComponentName)` or `setClass(Context, Class))` method. A very common use of this approach is to launch internal application activities.

Implicit intents on the other hand are sent to the system as requests and must carry enough information within them for the system to determine the component that can service the intent. If there are more than one component that can service this type of intent, then Android passes the intent to the component either with the highest priority or the one selected by the user via a list of options.

Intent Filter

Intent filters are used to declare serviceable intents in Android. This information is then used by Android to search the right serving component for implicit intents. Any application component such as an activity, service, and so on, can declare its support for handling a specific intent by using the `intent-filter` tag within its manifest declaration.

The application component can accept an incoming intent by filtering on any or all of the following three components of an intent:

`action`
: String containing the supported action or the event that has occurred

`category`
: String containing additional information describing the supported categories of the intent

`data`
: The URI and mime type of the data that is supported by the application component

An example of an `intent-filter` tag is as follows:

```
<intent-filter>
        <action android:name="android.intent.action.MAIN" />
        <category android:name="android.intent.category.LAUNCHER" />
</intent-filter>
```

The intent filter specified here would enable an activity to be listed in the device's application list as a launch point for the application.

An intent fileter specifies the types of intents that an activity, service, or broadcast receiver can respond to. It declares the capabilities of its parent component—what an activity or service can do and what types of broadcasts a receiver can handle. It opens the component to receiving intents of the advertised type, while filtering out those that are not meaningful for the component.

```
<intent-filter
        android:icon="drawable resource"
        android:label="string resource"
        android:priority="integer" >
    . . .
</intent-filter>
```

Services

The Android framework offers an application component to start and maintain background operation while the application is not in the foreground. This helps facilitate a better user experience for our application. This mechanism is known as a *service*.

The background service can be declared in the Android manifest using the `service` tag. The name of the Java class that extends the `Service` class must be provided using the `android:name` attribute within the tag.

The manifest can also be used to indicate whether the service should be started within the same process as the application or in a different process. By default, the service is started within the same process as the application and runs within the main thread of the application.

An example of the `service` tag is as follows

```
<service android:name=".ExampleService" />
```

Since the default behavior of the service is that it will be run in *main UI thread* of the application, make sure no time consuming or blocking tasks are performed within the service. If there is a need for such a task, it would be wise to spawn a thread from the service and use that thread for blocking tasks.

Broadcast Receiver

A broadcast receiver is a component provided by the Android framework to support receiving intents by the application. The broadcast receiver, if declared within the manifest, would enable the intents to be received even if the application is not running.

The broadcast receiver can be declared in the manifest using the `receiver` tag.

The name of the Java class that extends the `BroadcastReceiver` class should be declared with the `android:name` attribute within the element.

The targeted intents that can be processed by the receiver can be filtered using the `intent-filter` tags as described earlier.

An example of a broadcast receiver to handle system boot event is as follows:

```
<receiver android:name=".BootReceiver"
        <intent-filter>
                <action android:name="android.intent.action.RECEIVE_BOOT_COMPLE-
TED" />
        </intent-filter>
</receiver>
```

 Listening for a *boot completed* event using the broadcast receiver in the manifest is the recommended way to start an application when the device boots up. This is not suitable for all applications; only essential applications that need to run all the time.

Specifying Compatible Device Configuration

An Android manifest allows an application to specify the list of hardware configurations that is needed to run properly. For example, an application might require a qwerty hard keyboard. This mechanism ensures that the application is not installed on devices without support for the required features.

The required features can be listed using the `uses-configuration` tag. Multiple use configuration tags can be used to list different combinations of system features that the application can support.

An example of a system requirement tag is as follows:

```
<uses-configuration
        android:reqHardKeyboard="true"
        android:reqKeyboardType="qwerty" />
```

Declaring Needed Device Features

In addition to the overall device configuration described previously, an application might require other hardware features for it to function properly. For example, the location feature would be required for a navigation application.

These types of individual feature requirements can be listed in the Android manifest using the `uses-feature` tag.

An example of the feature requirement listing in the application manifest is as follows:

```
<uses-feature
  android:name="android.hardware.location.gps"
  android:required="true" />
```

The `android:required` attribute is used to indicate whether the application should not be installed on a device if the feature is not supported.

The default value for this flag is `true` and so it needs to be explicitly set to `false` if the application can run without issues even if the feature is not available.

 The Google Play store will filter the application for the target device based on the **uses-configuration** and `uses-feature` tags and the **android:required** attribute in each tag. Developers should employ these settings carefully to ensure that the application is not filtered incorrectly.

Permissions

Any application that wants to access privileged information such as contacts or various hardware components, such as the SD card or camera, must declare their usage in the application manifest.

The Android application installer (PackageManager) uses this declaration to alert the user about the access permissions that the application is requesting.

The permissions can be listed in the manifest using the `uses-permission` tag.

An example of `uses-permission` declaration is as follows:

```
<uses-permission
  android:name="android.permission.ACCESS_FINE_LOCATION" />
```

SDK Version

Since there are multiple versions of the Android SDK available in the market at any given time, the application developer can use the Android manifest to target the application to a particular version of the SDK as the primary one.

The `uses-sdk` tag can be used for declaration of the information about the SDK versions. The primary version of the SDK can be set using the `android:targetSdkVersion` attribute.

The application can also specify a minimum version of the SDK below which the application is not expected to support. The `android:minSdkVersion` attribute of the `uses-sdk` can be used to declare this.

An example of the `uses-sdk` declaration is as follows:

```
<uses-sdk
    android:minSdkVersion="5"
    android:targetSdkVersion="11"/>
```

 Even though the **maxSdkVersion** attribute can be set in the Android manifest using the SDK version tag, it's a bad idea, as it could cause the application to be uninstalled if a system update upgrades the device OS version to a newer version.

Hands-on Coding: Hybrid Hello World! Application

In this section, we will build a sample application wherein the UI is implemented in HTML and rendered using a WebView. To get started, create a sample project using Eclipse or on the command line.

```
$ mkdir helloworld
$ cd helloworld
$ android create project -n HelloWorld -p ./ -t \
    android-14 -k com.helloworld --activity MainActivity
```

Once you execute the commands, an empty native *Hello World* application will be created for you. Change the AndroidManifest XML to include the INTERNET permission:

```
<?xml version="1.0" encoding="utf-8"?>
<manifest xmlns:android="http://schemas.android.com/apk/res/android"
    package="com.helloworld" >

    <uses-permission android:name="android.permission.INTERNET" />

    <application
        android:icon="@drawable/icon"
        android:label="HelloWorld" >
        <activity android:name="com.helloworld.MainActivity" >
            <intent-filter>
                <action android:name="android.intent.action.MAIN" />

                <category android:name="android.intent.category.LAUNCHER" />
            </intent-filter>
        </activity>
    </application>

</manifest>
```

Next, we will modify the layout resource file to specify a WebView in the view hierarchy. This layout resource will be set as a content view in the MainActivity class of the application.

```
<?xml version="1.0" encoding="utf-8"?>
<LinearLayout xmlns:android="http://schemas.android.com/apk/res/android"
```

```
        android:layout_width="fill_parent"
        android:layout_height="fill_parent"
        android:orientation="vertical" >

    <WebView
        android:id="@+id/WebView"
        android:layout_width="fill_parent"
        android:layout_height="fill_parent" />

</LinearLayout>
```

Open the *MainActivity.java* file, and change the code as follows:

```
package com.helloworld;

import com.helloworld.R;
import android.app.Activity;
import android.os.Bundle;
import android.WebKit.WebView;

public class MainActivity extends Activity {

        @Override
        public void onCreate(Bundle savedInstanceState) {
                super.onCreate(savedInstanceState);

                 // Set the content view for the activity as the 'main' layout
        resource.
                 // Calling this API will cause the resource to be inflated and
        view
                // hierarchy to created and associated with the activity.
                setContentView(R.layout.main);

                // Since our modified layout resource file contains a WebView,
                // find the instance of it for us to process it further.
                WebView webView = (WebView) findViewById(R.id.WebView);

                // Enable JavaScript
                webView.getSettings().setJavaScriptEnabled(true);

                // Load the entry point page into the webView.
                webView.loadUrl("file:///android_asset/index.html");
        }
}
```

Now let's look at the sample HTML page that will be rendered by the application.

```
<!DOCTYPE html>
<html>
<head>
<meta name="viewport" content="width=device-width,
        initial-scale=1.0,
        user-scalable=0,
        minimum-scale=1.0,
```

```
        maximum-scale=1.0">
<title>Hello World</title>
<style>
* {
        -webkit-tap-highlight-color: rgba(0, 0, 0, 0);
}

html {
        height: 100%;
}

html, body {
        margin: 0;
        padding: 0;
        overflow: hidden;
        -webkit-text-size-adjust: none;
        -webkit-user-select: none;
}

body {
        font-family: Helvetica, Arial, sans-serif;
        font-size: 100%;
        width: 100%;
        height: 100%;
}

article {
        display: -webkit-box;
        width: 100%;
        height: 100%;
        -webkit-box-orient: vertical;
}

article section.view {
        display: -webkit-box;
        width: 100%;
        height: 100%;
        -webkit-box-orient: vertical;
        -webkit-box-align: center;
        -webkit-box-pack: center;
}
</style>
</head>
<body>

<article>
        <section class="view">Hello world!</section>
</article>

</body>
</html>
```

Once you have made the changes in the files, compile and deploy the app using an emulator or device. Voila!, you have your first hybrid application on Android, shown in Figure 3-3.

Figure 3-3. Hybrid "Hello World" application

## CHAPTER 4

WebView, WebKit, and WebSettings

In this chapter, we will be introducing the WebView control and its capabilities. Web-View in Android is a wrapper around the WebKit rendering engine, and can be used to display web pages inside your application. As a developer, you can use this control to render any web page as part of your application. These pages can be local or can be consumed from the Web. We will be using the WebView control to host our hybrid application. Although WebView itself is very powerful, the current API support is restricted by various specifications from standards governing bodies and individual organizations. Hence, it is often necessary to extend the API set to allow hybrid applications to access to platform capabilities.

The WebView as a Web Browser

A WebView is often used to load HTML content within a native application. The Web-View enables you to embed a web browser, which does not have any chrome (browser) controls including window frames, menus, toolbars and scroll bars into your activity layout.

The WebView is capable of displaying online or offline web content within its layout using HTML5, JavaScript, and CSS technologies. It also includes standard browser features like history, zooming, JavaScript, rendering CSS, and so on.

The most common implementation is to facilitate advertisement loading from remote servers. WebView often comes in handy for rendering complex UI views. One good example is the Facebook and LinkedIn applications wherein the news feed is rendered using the WebView control.

For those of you who wish to dig deeper on the subject of WebView and its integration within Android, we recommend you to have a look at *WebView.java* located in the frameworks project in *base/core/Java/ android/WebKit*. In summary, you will notice that WebView is just a wrapper view, which holds the handle to the canvas on which Web-Kit can operate. For almost everything else, it is a pass through to a controller module that manages user interactions, user data, and web requests.

So What Is WebKit?

WebKit is a rendering engine library to render web pages in view and windows. It also features a framework to interact with user events such as following links on user clicks. WebKit has become the de facto standard for web browser engines on mobile devices.

WebKit applications behave as you would expect. The WebKit conveniently creates and manages all the views needed to handle different *MIME* types. When the user clicks on a link in a page, the WebKit automatically creates the views needed to display the next page. For more details on WebKit, please refer to the WebKit website (*http://goo.gl/ MczY2*).

WebKit is a part of the libraries layer in the Android platform architecture. To get more information about WebKit on Android, read Joe Bowser's Android WebKit Development - A Cautionary Tale Presentation 1 (*http://goo.gl/j6m2q*).

 Since the Webkit is an open source browser engine, each mobile OS manufacturer might maintain a different version of WebKit. For example, WebKit in an iOS device is different from in an Android device. Check your WebKit HTML5 capabilities by visiting the html5test website (*http://goo.gl/brini*); here you'll find the available HTML5 APIs as well as CSS3 support.

Requesting Internet Permission from Android Manifest

In case, you want to load a URL in the WebView, you need to declare a uses-permission element just above the <application> ... </application> element in the *AndroidManifest.xml* file. In Chapter 3, the necessary application-specific permissions are explained in detail.

```xml
<?xml version="1.0" encoding="utf-8"?>
<manifest ... >
    <uses-permission android:name="android.permission.INTERNET" />
        <application> ... </application>
```

```
    ...
</manifest>
```

Instantiating and Accessing the WebView Control

A layout denotes the visual structure of an application screen. To use a WebView in your application, we need to add the WebView control to the view hierarchy of the application. This can be done in one of two ways:

- Using the XML-based layout files
- Programmatically

The XML way is preferred for many developers because it is not only easy to write but also because it can be done visually using the *Eclipse XML Graphical Layout Editor*. To add a WebView in a view hierarchy, add the following XML tag in your layout's XML.

```
<WebView xmlns:android="http://schemas.android.com/apk/res/android"
    android:id="@+id/WebView"
    android:layout_width="fill_parent"
    android:layout_height="fill_parent" />
```

A view created this way will be inflated (instantiated) by Android upon a user's call to setContentView() API. You can obtain handle to the WebView as you do with other views using the findViewById() API.

```
WebView webView = (WebView) findViewById(R.id.WebView);
```

Alternatively, you can create an and add a WebView to the application view hierarchy programmatically, as follows:

```
WebView WebView = new WebView(this);
contentView.addView(webView);
```

Loading a Web Page

Once you have a created a WebView control, you can request it to load a web page by using the loadURL() API passing the requested URL in the function argument. WebView supports loading resources from the Web or locally from the assets or resource folder.

- Root path to the *asset* folder in Android is *file:///android_asset*
- Root path to the *res* folder in Android is *file:///android_res*

Please note, that the url is *file:///android_asset* and not *file:///android_assets*. This is one of the most common mistakes made by developers during development.

 file:/// simply denotes that you wish to access the local filesystem, and points to the root directory. Anything mentioned after this is the relative path to the resource we would like to load in the WebView. Hence, when the URL is of the form *file:///android_asset*, we are specifying the base URL for the path to the *asset* folder for the application package.

```
// load index.html from the assets folder
WebView.loadUrl("file:///android_asset/index.html");

// load logo.png from the res folder
WebView.loadUrl("file:///android_res/drawable/logo.png");

// load a web based URL, Oreilly's homepage in this case
WebView.loadUrl("http://www.oreilly.com");
```

Loading HTML into WebView

You can request the WebView to render any valid HTML as a string using the `loadData()` method.

Let's look at the `loadData()` API in a bit more detail:

```
loadData(String data, String mimeType, String encoding)
```

`data` specifies the data to be loaded, HTML markup in our case, into the WebView using the data URL scheme. The data URL scheme allows us to include data inline in web pages as if they were external resources. Using this technique, we can load normally separate elements such as images and stylesheets in a single HTTP request rather than multiple HTTP requests.

`mimeType` will denote the data type, which will be `text/html`.

The `encoding` parameter specifies whether the data is base64 or URL encoded. If the data is base64 encoded, the value of the encoding parameter must be `base64`. For all other values of the parameter, including null, it is assumed that the data uses ASCII encoding for octets inside the range of safe URL characters.

```
String data = "<!DOCTYPE html>";
data += "<head><title>Hello World</title></head>";
data += "<body>Welcome to the WebView</body>";
data += "</html>";
// args: data, mimeType, encoding
WebView.loadData(data, "text/html", "UTF-8");
```

the above API will be used to create a data URL of the form `data:[<MIME-type>]` `[;charset=<encoding>][;base64],<data>` before it is loaded inside the WebView.

 If you would like to reference a file from an arbitrary source like the *res/drawable* directory within your HTML documents, using something like:

```
// Bad example
String data = "<!DOCTYPE html>";
data += "<head><title>THIS WILL NOT WORK</title></head>";
data += "<body><img src=\"file:///android_res/drawable/logo.png
\" /></body>";
data += "</html>";
WebView.loadData(data, "text/html", "UTF-8");
```

This code will not load the *logo.png* image, as JavaScript's *same origin policy* restricts all the resources on the web page to originate from the same site—in this case, `data:[<MIME-type>]` and not *file:///*, as we have requested.

To avoid this restriction, Google recommends using `loadDataWithBa seURL()` with an appropriate base URL, which is used both to resolve relative URLs and when applying JavaScript's same origin policy.

WebViewClient

Android's WebView is extensible and implements a number of delegatory classes including WebViewClient and WebChromeClient, which can be used by developers to customize the default behavior of WebView and inject data in the request/response call flows.

WebViewClient is a class that the WebView refers to before it handles everything that, in some way, is related to the rendering of a page. Using this class, you can add callback methods that are invoked to inform you of changes in the rendering.

These callbacks include:

- Start and stop loading of web requests
- Whether the browser should load specific resources
- Notify errors, login requests, and form resubmissions

Android WebView has a default implementation of the WebViewClient, which can be overridden by the default delegate using the `setWebViewClient()` method of the WebView.

```
webView.setWebViewClient(new WebViewClient(webView) {
  // override all the methods
});
```

WebChromeClient

WebChromeClient is also a delegate class, responsible for everything browser UI specific, unlike the WebViewClient, which is responsible for everything that is related to the rendering of the web content.

The WebChromeClient lets you handle the browser's visited history, create new windows, take care of alerts, prompts, and console messages. A simple application with no requirements on the integration will be fine without overriding the default WebChromeClient delegate. You can specify your own delegate using the `setWebChromeClient()` method of the WebView.

```
webView.setWebChromeClient(new WebChromeClient(webView){
  // override all the methods
});
```

Loading Local Files into the WebView

Android WebView provides a very flexible set of APIs to load documents from multiple sources. However, you may have to tweak the behavior of the WebView in certain cases, as the same origin policy would restrict the locations from which the content can be loaded within the web browser—for example, loading a local file on the filesystem.

In the following sections, we will look at some of the techniques you can use to allow the web browser to load content from multiple sources.

Load local files from *res/drawable* into the WebView with a given base URL:

```
String html = "<!DOCTYPE html>";
html += "<head><title>Loading files from res/drawable directory</title></head>";
html += "<body><img src=\"logo.png\" />/body>";
html += "</html>";
WebView.loadDataWithBaseURL("file:///android_res/drawable/", html, "text/html",
"UTF-8", null);
```

Load local files from an SD card into the WebView without a given base URL:

```
String base = Environment.getExternalStorageDirectory().getAbsolutePath()
        .toString();
String imagePath = "file://"+ base + "/logo.png";
String html = "<!DOCTYPE html>";
html += "<head><title>Loading files from SDCard</title></head>";
html += "<body><img src=\""+ imagePath + "\" />/body>";
html += "</html>";
WebView.loadDataWithBaseURL("", html, "text/html","UTF-8", null);
```

One important thing to note is that the previous solution is supported only in API Level 2.2 and above. If you are using an API level lower
than 2.2, an alternative solution can be executed by reading the file
into a string buffer explicitly.

Load local files into the WebView by reading the contents of the file in Java and then
passing the data to the WebView:

```
// Load an html file
String html = loadFileFromSDCard("file:///sdcard/oreilly/book/logo.png");
WebView.loadDataWithBaseURL("", html, "text/html", "UTF-8", null);
```

or:

```
// Load an image file
String pngData = loadFileFromAssets("file:///android_asset/images/logo.png");
WebView.loadData(pngData, "image/png", "UTF-8");
```

Load Flash Files into the WebView

In order to load flash files from SDCard into the view, you can link your flash files in
the embed tag using *file:///* protocol.

```
<!-- flash.html -->
<html>
  <head>
    <title>Playing Flash movie</title>
  </head>
  <body>
    <object width="200" height="200">
      <param name="movie" value="hybrid.swf">
      <embed src="file:///sdcard/hybrid.swf" width="200" height="200"></embed>
    </object>
  </body>
</html>
```

Then, you need to load your *flash.html* file from *SDCard* using the loadUrl() method.

```
String base = Environment.getExternalStorageDirectory().getAbsolutePath().to-
String();
String html = "file://" + base + "/flash.html";
if (Environment.getExternalStorageState().equals(Environment.MEDIA_MOUNTED)) {
    WebView.loadUrl(html);
}
```

Reading Files from the res/raw Directory

If you need to read a file (e.g., *home.html*) from the *res/raw* directory and display it in
the WebView, you need to pass the resource ID (e.g., *R.raw.home*) to your reader function in order to get it as string.

```
WebView.loadData(getRawFileFromResource(R.raw.home), "text/html", "UTF-8");

private String getRawFileFromResource(int resourceId) {
        StringBuilder sb = new StringBuilder();
        Scanner s = new Scanner(getResources().openRawResource(resourceId));
        while (s.hasNextLine()) {
                sb.append(s.nextLine() + "\n");
        }
        return sb.toString();
}
```

Triggering JavaScript Functions from the Java Layer

A key aspect of an hybrid application would be its ability to allow native code to call JavaScript APIs, for delivering data, callbacks, and events. Since, there is no direct API for this in WebKit, developers often use the `loadUrl()` function for this purpose. The `loadURL()` function requests the WebView to load and execute the specified URL.

If you recall the structure of a URL, it looks something like:

```
scheme: [hostaddress][params]
  |         |            |        |
 |protocol| optional    |        |
 -------- |address for  |        |
          | service     |        |
          -------------- params|
```

The protocol can be any valid scheme as long as there is either a valid default handler registered in WebKit for that scheme or your application serves this scheme. Examples for protocol would be http, https, ftp, JavaScript, or karura (*karura://karura.js*)—in our case, identifying our declared protocol scheme.

The JavaScript protocol is of special interest to us for this topic. The syntax for the JavaScript protocol is `JavaScript:sScript`.

This protocol scheme is used to specify a sequence of JavaScript statements to be executed by the JavaScript engine within the browser context. This is often handy in specifying event handlers for UI controls within the web page. When a browser engine is requested to browse to a JavaScript URL, it will execute the accompanying JavaScript without reloading the DOM. This is a very important feature in modern web browsers. We will use this design pattern to pass parameters from Java across to JavaScript. This is how it is done:

1. Create a string buffer to represent the JavaScript that you wish to call.

2. Prepend the JavaScript protocol scheme to this string.

3. Call `loadURL()`, passing the string as the argument.

For example, if we wish to display an alert dialog in the WebView, as a result of some Java code execution, we would write something like:

```
String js = "alert('Alert from Java');";
WebView.loadUrl("JavaScript:" + js);
```

Opening a WebView in Fullscreen Mode

At times, you may want to display a fullscreen WebView to the user. Although you can request the WebView to cover the entire activity, by default, the activity does not cover the full screen, and you will observe a title bar and a notification bar. You can make an activity a fullscreen activity by either specifying activity flags in the manifest file or by doing it programatically.

Make an activity full screen through *AndroidManifest.xml*:

```
<?xml version="1.0" encoding="utf-8"?>
<manifest ... >
        <activity
            android:theme="@android:style/Theme.NoTitleBar.Fullscreen" >
                ...
        </activity>
</manifest>
```

Or make an activity fullscreen programmatically:

```
@Override
public void onCreate(Bundle savedInstanceState) {
        super.onCreate(savedInstanceState);
        requestWindowFeature(Window.FEATURE_NO_TITLE);
        getWindow().setFlags(WindowManager.LayoutParams.FLAG_FULLSCREEN,
                WindowManager.LayoutParams.FLAG_FULLSCREEN);
        setContentView(R.layout.main);
        ...
}
```

When you set your activity to fullscreen mode, the `resize` event is not fired when the soft keyboard comes out in the WebView. We have done numerous experiments to capture the `resize` event from JavaScript, but with no luck. This could be Android limitation or a bus. This issue has been raised to Android developers at Google. The alternative solution of how to mitigate this issue is addressed in the next section.

Enabling a Resize Event in JavaScript While Your Application Is Fullscreen

To enable a resize event while your application is fullscreen, do the following:

- Use the *res/values/styles.xml* file to make your application fullscreen and turn off the window title.

```xml
<?xml version="1.0" encoding="utf-8"?>
<resources>

    <style name="Theme" parent="android:Theme.Light">
        <item name="android:textViewStyle">@style/Theme.TextView</item>
        <item name="android:windowTitleStyle">@style/WindowTitle</item>
        <item name="android:windowContentOverlay">@null</item>
        <item name="android:windowNoTitle">true</item>
    </style>

    <style name="WindowTitle" parent="@android:style/Theme">
        <item name="android:textSize">10sp</item>
        <item name="android:textColor">@android:color/white</item>
    </style>

    <style name="Theme.TextView" parent="@android:style/Widget.TextView">
        <item name="android:textSize">10sp</item>
        <item name="android:textColor">@android:color/black</item>
    </style>

</resources>
```

- Apply this theme to your application using the following XML attribute in your manifest.

```xml
<application
        android:icon="@drawable/icon"
        android:label="Demo"
        android:theme="@style/Theme" > ... </application>
```

- You can now capture the `resize` event in your HTML.

```javascript
$(window).bind('resize', function() {
        console.error('onResize');
});
```

Binding Java Objects to WebView Using the addJavaScriptInterface() Method

The WebView allows developers to extend the JavaScript API namespace by defining their own components in Java and then making them available in the JavaScript environment. This technique comes in handy when you wish to access a platform feature not already available in JavaScript or wish to consume a component written in Java through JavaScript.

The addJavaScriptInterface() method of the WebView can be used for this purpose.

```
JavaScriptInterface JavaScriptInterface = new JavaScriptInterface(this);
myWebView = new MyWebView(this);
myWebView.addJavaScriptInterface(JavaScriptInterface, "HybridNote");
```

In this example, JavaScriptInterface is bound to the JavaScript environment of Web-View and is accessible using the HybridNote object (aka *namespace*). Depending upon the Android version, either all public or some special methods of the bound objects will be accessible inside the JavaScript code. Once the object is added to the WebView using the function specified earlier, the object will be available to JavaScript only after the page in the WebView is loaded next or the existing page is reloaded. This can be achieved by calling the loadData() function of the WebView object.

 Although addJavaScriptInterface() is powerful for building hybrid apps, using this method presents a wide range of security issues because the same-origin policy (SOP) does not apply to this method, and third-party JavaScript libraries or an untrusted child iframe from a different domain may access those exposed methods in the Java layer. As a result of this, attackers can take advantage of an XSS vulnerability and execute native code or inject malicious code into your application.

From the JavaScript layer, all the public methods of the exposed Java objects can be accessed in Android versions below Jelly Bean MR1 (API Level - 17). For Jelly Bean MR1 API Level and above, exposed functions should specifically be annotated with @JavaScriptInterface to prevent any unwanted methods from being exposed.

The JavaScript layer does not have direct access to the exposed Java object's fields. If needed, explicit getters and setters must be provided for accessing the fields.

@JavaScriptInterface Annotations

If you set your targetSdkVersion to 17 (or higher) in *AndroidManifest.xml* all the methods that are accessed by JavaScript must have @JavaScriptInterface annotations.

```
import android.WebKit.javaScriptInterface;

// SDK version 17 or above.
@JavaScriptInterface
public void showToast(String toast)  {
        // show toast...
}
```

In Android 2.3, the addJavaScriptInterface() method does not work as expected. However, given *2.3* is still the most used version of Android, you may want your application to work on 2.3 devices as well.

Developers across the Web have come up with a number of workarounds to take care of this. You can find one such implementation at Android 2.3 WebView's broken Add-JavascriptInterface website (*http://goo.gl/EICOa*).

Another approach is to use an `onJsPrompt()` callback. Wherein the `message` or the `defaultValue` parameter can be used to pass the name of the method to be executed in the native environment along with params.

```
@Override
public boolean onJsPrompt(WebView view, String url, String message,
        String defaultValue, JsPromptResult result) {

    // Check the url to ensure that the request originated from
    // whitelisted source

    // Check to see if message or defaultValue contain JavaScript request.
    if (defaultValue.startsWith("karura:")) {
            // process the request
    } else{
            // display the confirmation dialog to the user if required
    }

    return trueOrFalse; // based on whether you handled the notification
}
```

Security Considerations for Hybrid Applications

In Android versions before 4.2 (Jelly Bean, `targetSdkVersion` 17), the JavaScript layer, upon getting access to the exposed Java object, can access all of the object's public members using *reflection*. Reflection is a powerful set of APIs, commonly used by programs that require the ability to examine or modify the runtime behavior of applications running in the Java Virtual Machine.

For platforms before API level 17, you can use reflection inside of JavaScript by calling something like:

```
function execute(cmdArgs) {
        boundObj.getClass().forName("Java.lang.Runtime").getMethod("getRuntime",
                null).invoke(null,null).exec(cmdArgs);
}

var p = execute(["/data/data/com.yourapp/malicious-app"]);
document.write(getContents(p.getInputStream()));
```

This could allow an attacker to run malicious Java code in the host application's context, which could pose a security risk.

As an application developer, care must be taken to ensure that we expose the Java object to WebView only as necessary, especially in the case of running JavaScript from untrusted sources such as external websites and so on.

For increased security, you should also load all the external JavaScript files over the Secure Sockets Layer (SSL) protocol. Any exceptions to this should be explicitly reviewed and approved by you.

HttpOnly Cookies and the Secure Flag

Cookies are one of the most common ways developers store application data. Among other things, it is used to remember the state of the web application in the previous run. Access to this data by untrusted JavaScript could pose a huge risk to your application. To prevent this, you can make your cookies HttpOnly in the HTTP response.

The HttpOnly cookie flag became a standard with the RFC #6265 document that can be found at the ietf.org website (*http://goo.gl/RRHSC*).

An HttpOnly flagged cookie cannot be stolen easily via non-HTTP methods, such as JavaScript or Flash using document.cookie as a pervasive attack technique.

Here's an example of how the HttpOnly attribute is visible in the HTTP headers:

```
HTTP/1.1 200 OK
Content-Type: text/html; charset=utf-8
Set-Cookie: id=cdb6352b48e62e0691efe552e3e4cecb; path=/; HttpOnly
```

If you use the SSL protocol for delivering your web content and need to set cookies using JavaScript, then you need to enable the secure flag in your cookie function in order to set a secure cookie.

```
document.cookie = "name=value; expires=date; path=path; domain=domain; secure";
```

 On the Android developer website, there are great tips about WebView security. For additional information, please refer to the Android WebView API website (*http://goo.gl/xJTvO*).

Domain Whitelisting

You can create an allowed list of domains that WebView can view if your application needs to navigate to domains outside the expected domain. Just use the shouldOverri deUrlLoading(WebView view, String url) method:

```
@Override
public boolean shouldOverrideUrlLoading(WebView view, String url) {
        if (!Uri.parse(url).getHost().equals("www.oreilly.com")) {
                return false;
        }
        view.loadUrl(url);
        return true;
}
```

However, restricting loading remote resources within the shouldOverrideUrlLoading(WebView view, String url) method does not intercept the requests that are made from IFRAME, XmlHttpRequests Ajax Object, and SRC attributes in HTML tags.

A solution to the problem mentioned in the Warning would be to intercept the request and manually load different content into this view.

```
@Override
public WebResourceResponse shouldInterceptRequest(WebView view, String url) {
        if (url.contains(".js")) {
                String str = "alert('This is a replaced JavaScript code.')";
                InputStream is = null;
                try {
                        is = new ByteArrayInputStream(str.getBytes("UTF8"));
                } catch (UnsupportedEncodingException e) {
                        e.printStackTrace();
                }
                String type = "application/JavaScript";
                return new WebResourceResponse(type, "UTF-8", is);
        }
        return super.shouldInterceptRequest(view, url);
}
```

Configuring WebView Settings with WebSettings

WebView in Android, provides a very comprehensive configuration interface, WebSettings, which can be used to customize the behavior of the WebView at runtime. The WebSettings object is valid only during the lifecycle of a WebView. In other words, an IllegalStateException will be thrown if you try to access any method from a WebView.getSettings() object if a WebView is already destroyed.

You can retrieve WebSettings with WebView.getSettings() API.

```
WebView WebView = new WebView(this);
WebSettings settings = WebView.getSettings();
```

Preventing Local Files from Being Loaded in the WebView

The setAllowFileAccess() API allows developers to control access to local files by the WebView. This API is one of several WebView settings you can configure at runtime. By default, this setting is enabled for accessing files in the filesystem. This setting does not restrict the WebView to load local resources from the *file:///android_asset* (assets) and *file:///android_res* (resources) directories. For security reasons, if your app does not require access to the filesystem, it is a good practice to turn this setting off.

```
settings.setAllowFileAccess(false);
```

Enabling JavaScript

For security reasons, JavaScript is *disabled* in the WebView by default. You can enable/disable JavaScript using `setJavaScriptEnabled()` method.

```
settings.setJavaScriptEnabled(true);
```

We suggest that you always include all the JavaScript libraries in the *assets* directory of your application within your hybrid app.

If you are using third-party JavaScript libraries in your application, eventually, your application will inherit all the bugs and vulnerabilities that may cause undesired situations for your application. Some developers prefer downloading third-party JavaScript from their own web servers to mitigate the risks of being hacked. This allows them to react more quickly than others in removing the malicious code from the web server.

Again, ideally, you should deliver all your JavaScript files within your application.

Turning on some of the WebView settings unnecessarily may result in unexpected behavior in your application. Hence, it is a good practice to turn off features not required by your application.

For example, if you are not using a Flash plug-in, turn it off using the `setPlugin State(PluginState.OFF)` method, which may prevent attackers from compromising your app via third-party plug-ins.

```
WebView WebView = new WebView(this);
WebSettings settings = WebView.getSettings();
settings.setPluginState(PluginState.OFF);
```

We encourage you to read the following research papers published by Syracuse University in New York:

Visit the "Attacks on WebView in the Android Systems" article (*http://goo.gl/LyPev*).

Visit the "Touchjacking Attacks on Web in Android, iOS, and Windows Phone" article (*http://goo.gl/i89Sn*).

As an Android developer, you should always follow the best practices of different remediation and mitigation strategies for your mobile app.

Setting Default Font Size

By default, the WebKit renders and displays fonts in 16 sp (scale-independent pixels) unit. This unit enables WebView to adjust the font size for both screen density and the user's preference. If you would like to change the font size to something other than the default size, you can use the `setDefaultFontSize()` method with the preferred font size value.

```
WebView WebView = new WebView(this);
WebSettings settings = WebView.getSettings();
settings.setDefaultFontSize(20);
```

Zoom Controls

Setting the `setBuiltInZoomControls()` method to `false` will prevent the built-in zoom mechanisms. Setting this to `true` will allow the `setDisplayZoomControls()` method to show onscreen zoom controls. `setDefaultZoom(ZoomDensity.FAR)` sets the default zoom density of a web page. Setting its value to FAR makes it appear in 240 dpi at 100%. `setSupportZoom()` with `false` value will set whether the WebView should support zooming using its onscreen zoom controls and gestures or not.

From the user experience perspective, turning off zooming for the most of the mobile apps will be ideal for many users unless the application features require zooming.

```
WebView WebView = new WebView(this);
WebSettings settings = WebView.getSettings();
settings.setBuiltInZoomControls(false);
settings.setDefaultZoom(ZoomDensity.FAR);
settings.setSupportZoom(false);
```

Hardware Acceleration

Android uses some form of hardware accelerated drawing since version 1.0, basically, for compositing windows. However, the local window changes are done in software. Historically, the Android browser used a rendering technique optimized for minimizing errors, not speed of rendering. Starting at version 3.0, Android introduced full hardware acceleration for applications. This is not enabled by default for applications targeted for platforms below version 4.0. The web browser itself moved to a *tile-based rendering architecture* as opposed to display list architecture, which makes it more responsive.

If you wish to enable hardware acceleration in your application or activity, you can set `android:handwareAccelerated="true"` in your manifest.

```
// enable hardware acceleration using code (>= level 11)
if (Build.VERSION.SDK_INT >= Build.VERSION_CODES.HONEYCOMB) {
    WebView.setLayerType(View.LAYER_TYPE_HARDWARE, null);
}
```

```
settings.setRenderPriority(WebSettings.RenderPriority.HIGH);
settings.setCacheMode(WebSettings.LOAD_NO_CACHE);
```

 If you enable hardware acceleration for your application, make sure you test it. Enabling hardware acceleration has side-effects, the most important one being that it adds a significant amount of memory requirements to your application (approx. 7-8M at minimum). This can have huge impact on low end devices.

Given that the Android ecosystem is so heavily fragmented, it is possible that you may observe issues with hardware-accelerated WebView. To selectively turn off hardware acceleration for your WebView, you can either set it to `android:handwareAcceler ated="false"` for the entire application or the activity hosting the WebView in the application manifest file.

You can achieve the same effect programmatically using the following code:

```
// selectively disable hardware acceleration for WebView
// honeycomb (3.0) and higher
if (Build.VERSION.SDK_INT >= Build.VERSION_CODES.HONEYCOMB) {
        WebView.setLayerType(View.LAYER_TYPE_SOFTWARE, null);
}
```

## CHAPTER 5

Inter-workings of the JavaScript and Java Layers

Now that we have looked at each individual piece, let's put it all together and look at the end-to-end architecture of a hybrid application.

Architecture of a Hybrid Application

Hybrid applications are special, bringing together best of both worlds to an extent. Architecturally, an hybrid application would look like Figure 5-1.

A sufficiently complex hybrid application would typically contain most of the components identified in Figure 5-1, although not necessarily. Let's quickly go over these components before we delve into more details.

WebView

> A hybrid application is a primarily a web app with access to platform capabilities through an additional set of user defined APIs. This web application requires a WebView to render content and host the business logic.

View, model, and controller

> Since the application is primarily written in JavaScript, depending upon the JavaScript library you use, you will have some form of implementation of model, view, and controller components.

JS-Java Bridge

> It is the glue layer that allows the native and web environments to interact with each other. The bridge should allow for execution of *synchronous* and *asynchronous* APIs. As was discussed in the previous chapters, this layer is one of the most crucial layers in a hybrid application for several reasons, including performance, ease of use, and security.

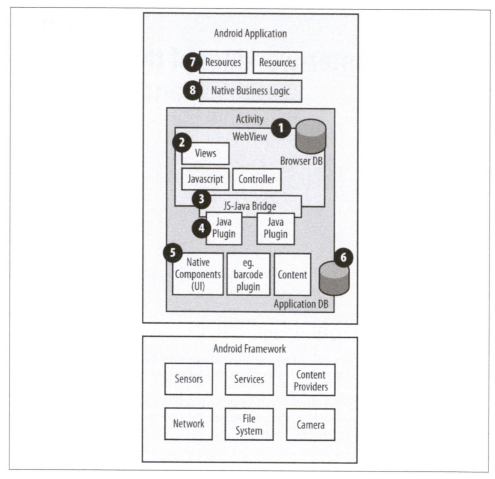

Figure 5-1. Hybrid application architecture

Java plug-ins

A Java plug-in is the user defined extension API that has been exposed to the Java-Script environment.

Native components

These are native services and components you wish to access as part of your hybrid applications. Some of the examples include showing `actionbar`, native dialogs, accessing location, and so on.

Application data

While HTML5 data storage gives us some capabilities to store data, you may often want to store BLOBs in custom formats; this is where application data, filesystem APIs, and native APIs come into play.

Assets and resources

Assets and resources contain the static artifacts that ship with your application. You can use resources to localize text if you like.

Native business logic

One very important architectural split while designing hybrid applications is the split for the business logic between the native and web components. Often you may feel the need to implement part of the business logic in the native layer for several reasons, including access to native components, additional security, or just that a particular component you wish to link to is only available in the native layer.

Calling Java Methods from JavaScript

WebKit and the WebView allow developers to bind Java objects to JavaScript objects. Using this bridge, the bound object can access the Java APIs from JavaScript. One important thing to remember is that the bound JavaScript alias is a global variable, and can be accessed anywhere within the app.

The `addJavaScriptInterface()` API available in the WebView can be used to bind a Java object to a JavaScript alias at runtime. Let's look at what happens when an object is bound; see Figure 5-2.

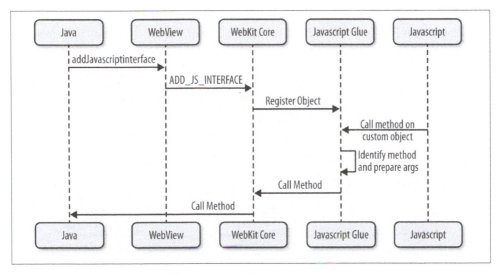

Figure 5-2. Binding a Java object to JavaScript

The object binding framework available as part of Android is very flexible and powerful. It is intelligent in the sense that it can automatically bind return objects for Java method calls for them to be accessible in the JavaScript environment. Unlike their explicit counterparts, the implicitly bound objects are anonymous objects and would be lost unless you store an explicit reference to them in JavaScript variables.

```
class MyLocationProvider {
        Location getLocation();
}

    WebView.addJavaScriptInterface(myLocationProvider, "nativeLocProvider");
```

In the previous example, `nativeLocProvider` is global and can be accessed anywhere within the JavaScript.

```
var location = nativeLocProvider.getLocation();
```

In the second example, when we call `getLocation` in JavaScript, the return object is automatically bound to the JavaScript environment, however, as shown earlier we will have to maintain a reference to the returned object to refer to it in the future.

As with any programming paradigm, the Java plug-in APIs, available through the bound native object can be both synchronous or asynchronous. Just to put things in perspective, a synchronous API will block the caller until it returns. An asynchronous API, on the other hand, does not block the caller and typically will require a callback that will be executed once the work is complete.

Synchronous APIs

The diagram in Figure 5-3 illustrates the control flow for a synchronous function.

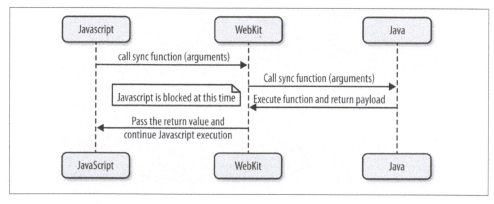

Figure 5-3. Synchronous API execution

Asynchronous APIs

Asynchronous APIs usually involve a callback function being called to inform the caller about the status of its request, successful or otherwise. At times, multiple callbacks may be involved depending upon the complexity; see Figure 5-4.

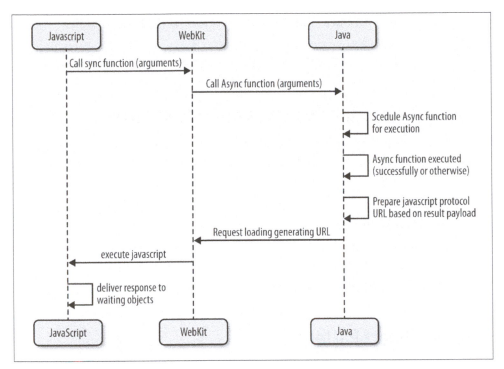

Figure 5-4. Asynchronous API execution

This brings us to our next topic, calling JavaScript methods from Java.

Calling JavaScript Methods from Java

Calling JavaScript methods from Java is not as straightforward as accessing a Java method from JavaScript. JavaScript objects are not exposed in the Java layer. The way you call a JavaScript function is by creating a JavaScript URL, which is then passed onto the WebView for execution. There are a couple of technical fallouts of this approach. The first being that you have to be aware of the JavaScript runtime code structure, and second, you must ensure that the JavaScript URL has proper error handling defined as part of the JavaScript. The JavaScript URL can be passed onto the WebView, and hence the JavaScript environment, using `loadURL()` (or similar) API. Also note that the Java-Script receiver object has to be made addressable from the Java layer. You can do this by either making the scope of these variables global or by building some form of dispatcher framework that can route the response to a correct receiver object.

The reasons behind this rather complex marshaling of data back from Java to JavaScript are:

- JavaScript is single-threaded, hence, calling into JavaScript would involve marshaling the response parameters to the thread hosting the JavaScript engine.
- The JavaScript URL approach has long existed and appears to be a perfect candidate solution for this, instead of developing a completely new API.

Routing Data to the Correct JavaScript Receiver

In the previous section, we touched upon needing a form of routing framework for delivering responses from Java to the correct JavaScript objects. There are several ways you can achieve this.

- If you use an existing hybrid application framework like PhoneGap, Cordova, or Karura, then this is already done for you.
- You can use some of the existing asynchronous function framework available in JavaScript—for example, the Deferred Object framework available in jQuery.
- Build a custom framework yourself.

Deferred Object Pattern

The Deferred Object pattern is the key pattern used by a number of JavaScript applications for decoupling of the request from the code that handles the results of the request and allows multiple callbacks to be attached upon notification of a result. To achieve such a decoupling, the Deferred Object provides functions that allow the callback functions to be registered for handling the success, failure, or the progress of the request. Deferred Object framework is available as part of the jQuery library.

Here's how to create a deferred object in jQuery:

```
var deferred = $.Deferred();
// var deferred =  new Deferred();
// var deferred = jQuery.Deferred();
```

Register Success Callback Using deferred.done()

The `.done()` function allows a callback function to be registered with the Deferred Object. This callback function will be called once the request is successfully completed when `.resolve()` is called on the Deferred Object.

```
deferred.done(function(data) {
        console.log("Success callback: " + data);
});
```

Register Failure Callback Using deferred.fail()

The `.fail()` function allows the registration of a callback that will be called if the request fails with any error when `.reject()` is called on the Deferred Object. The function can provide the appropriate error code and message that describes the error encountered.

```
deferred.fail(function(errCode, errMsg) {
        console.log("Failure callback: " + errCode + " - " + errMsg);
});
```

Register Progress Callback Using deferred.progress()

The `.progress()` function provides the option to update the caller of the progress of the request. The callback function can be called multiple times during the lifetime of the request while `.notify()` is being called on the Deferred Object. In contrast, the `.done()` and `.fail()` callbacks are executed only once per lifecycle of the request.

```
deferred.progress(function(percentage) {
        console.log("Progress callback: " + percentage);
});
```

Simpler Callback registration with .then()

The `.then()` function provides a convenient way to specify the success, fail, and progress callback functions in one place. All of the callback parameters are optional, which allows the developer to declare the callbacks only for the functions that are of interest. The `.then()` function is fired when the `.resolve()` or `.reject()` functions are called on the Deferred Object.

The structure of the `deferred.then()` function is as follows:

```
deferred.then(successCallback, failCallback, progressCallback);
```

Combining the example given for `.done()`, `.fail()`, and `.progress()`, to use the `.then()` function, we would be able to achieve an equivalent behavior as shown here:

```
deferred.then(function() {
        console.log("Success callback");
}, function(errCode, errMsg) {
        console.log("Failure callback: " + errCode + " - " + errMsg);
}, function() {
        console.log("Progress callback");
});
```

Synchronizing Multiple Asynchronous Events with $.when()

You can also synchronize one or more events using deferred's $.when() helper function, as in the following example. The $.when() function waits for all its tasks to be executed, and once supplied deferred events are resolved, depending on the events' success and failure states, .then() or .fail() callbacks will be fired. If one of the tasks fails, then .fail() will be invoked.

```
function doThis() {
    return $.get('this.html');
}

function doThat() {
    return $.get('that.html');
}

$.when(doThis(), doThat()).then(function(data) {
        console.log("Both events are successful.");
}).fail(function(errCode, errMsg) {
        console.log("One or more events are failed.");
});
```

Resolve a Deferred Object

The potential of the Deferred Object is seen by allowing the success callback(s) to be called when the request is completed successfully.

The Deferred Object can be used to invoke the success callback(s) by calling the .re solve() function on the Deferred Object. The .resolve() function can be used to provide the callback function(s) with the arguments that communicate the artifacts of the request.

```
var deferred =  new Deferred();

// register the success callback with two args
deferred.done(function(arg1, arg2) {
        alert("Success callback with two artifacts");
};
// Do some processing resulting in artifact1 and artifact2
```

```
              .
              .
              .
// Calling the resolve function on the Deferred Object with two artifacts as
// arguments will trigger the success callback to be called with the same.
deferred.resolve(artifact1, artifact2);
```

Reject a Deferred Object

Similarly, the other important usage of the Deferred Object is to notify any interested parties to the failure of an async request.

The Deferred Object can be used to invoke the failure callback(s) by calling the .reject() function on the Deferred Object. Similar to the success callback, the .reject() function can be used to provide the failure callback(s) with error codes and error messages that describe the cause of the failure.

```
var deferred =  new Deferred();

// register the failure callback with the errorCode and errorMsg args
deferred.fail(function(errorCode, errorMsg) {
        alert("Failure callback: " +errorCode+ " & message" + errorMsg);
};
// Do some processing resulting in an error with errCode and corresponding
// error message errMsg
              .
              .
// Calling the reject function on the Deferred Object with the error code
// and err message would be passed back to the callback function(s) that
// have been registered.
deferred.reject(errCode, errMsg);
```

Use of Promise

A typical usage of a Deferred Object pattern would be to provide the caller of a function with a handle to a Deferred Object. The caller can use the handle to set the callbacks that it is interested in.

In addition, the function that created the Deferred Object would want to restrict the ability to finalize the Deferred Object by calling .resolve() or .reject(), to only itself or its downstream functions.

Both the requirements are supported in the Deferred Object framework by the .promise() function. The .promise() function returns a Deferred Object that can be used only to set the callbacks but not call the functions that could alter the state of the object. The called function can return this to the caller, which can then set the callback functions required upon the Deferred action completion.

For example, consider an Ajax request to download a web page. The call flow showing the usage of promise is as follows:

```
function ajaxRequest(url) {
        var deferred =  new Deferred();

        // Initiate the request to download url and pass the
        // Deferred Object to enable the downstream downloader
        // to call resolve() or reject() and progress() as necessary
        download(url, deferred);

        // Return the Deferred Promise Object to enable the
        // callbacks to be set by the caller
        return deferred.promise();
}

function caller() {
        ajaxRequest("http://oreilly.com")then(function() {
                alert("Page successfully downloaded");
        }, function(errCode, errorMsg) {
                alert("Failure Callback: " + errCode + " - " + errorMsg);
        }, function() {
                console.log("Progress update called");
        });
}
```

Use of deferred.progress()

In addition to using the Deferred Object to indicate success or failure of the request, it can be used to indicate the status of the request as well. The callback function that needs to be provided with the status update of the request can be registered using the .pro gress() or using the third parameter of the .then() function.

To be able to update the status by calling the progress callback registered, the Deferred Object provides the .notify() function that takes the progress update parameters as arguments. For example, this callback can be used to update the UI elements such as the progress bar for providing feedback to the user.

```
function progressBar() {
    var deferred = $.Deferred();

    var i = 0;
    var intervalId = setInterval(function() {
        deferred.notify(++i);
        if (i == 99) {
                        clearInterval(intervalId);
                }
    }, 1000);

    return deferred.promise();
```

```
};

var promise = progressBar();

promise.progress(function(percentage) {
        console.log(percentage + "% completed");
});
```

The progress callback function can be called multiple times during the lifetime of the request. In contrast, the `deferred.resolve()` and `deferred.reject()` functions are only executed once per the lifecycle of the request.

In the following simple example, we can see the whole picture of how the Deferred Object is used.

```
function requestDB() {
        // 1 - create the Deferred
        var deferred = $.Deferred();

        XMLHttpRequest xhr = new XMLHttpRequest();
        xhr.open("GET", "/api/contact", true);
        xhr.addEventListener('load', function() {
                if (xhr.readyState == 4) {
                        if ((xhr.status >= 200 && xhr.status <= 300)
                                || xhr.status == 304) {
                                // 3a - triggers the .then() or
                                // .done() callbacks
                                var response = { name: "O'reilly" };
                                deferred.resolve(response);
                        } else {
                                // 3b - triggers the .fail() callback with
                                // an error code and a message
                                deferred.reject(404, "File not found.");
                        }
                }
        }, false);
        xhr.send();

        // 2 - return the promise right away
        return deferred.promise();
}

$.when(RequestDB()).then(function(response) {
        // 3a1 - access to returned parameters
        console.log(data.name);
}).fail(function(errCode, errMsg) {
        // 3b1 - access to fail messages
        console.log("Failure callback: " + errCode + " - " + errMsg);
});
```

When the `requestDB()` function is called by the `$.when()` function, there are four steps expected to happen:

1. We create a Deferred Object that can then facilitate callbacks to be fired based on the expected results from the program.

2. Once the Deferred Object is created, we return this object immediately so the consumer application can attach different utility functions, such as `.done()`, `.then()`, or `.fail()`, to handle its outcome.

3. If the application returns a result successfully from the source, then we have to let the consumer application know about this outcome. In this case, we call the `.re solve()` function with or without return parameter `response`.

    a. Once the Deferred Object resolves the result with a success outcome and passes any parameters to a handling function we can access these parameters (including the `response` parameter) from the anonymous callback functions in `.done()` or `.then()`. In our case, the `response` JSON object holds the return data, and we should be able to access the key/value pairs within the callback function.

    b. If the outcome results in a failure, we can also let the consumer application know about it. It is good practice to pass descriptive messages to the consumer application about what went wrong while processing the request. In our case, we pass an error code and a message to the consumer application to handle the result accordingly.

    c. if we receive a failure from our request, then the `.fail()` function is able to pass us the parameters that are dispatched from `.reject()`. In our case, we can access the error code and the message from our anonymous function in order to handle this failure with a friendlier error message to the users in the UI.

Cache Manager for Handling Multiple Deferred Objects

We need to keep track of which Deferred Objects need to be executed for a given handle key. Since the `$.Deferred` object allows multiple callbacks to be attached even after the callbacks are fired, it is necessary that we cache the deferred handles for all async tasks.

When we invoke a Java method from JavaScript, we pass this cache handle key along with the method ID and parameters so that Java resolves the content and calls back the JavaScript function with that handle key to invalidate it from the cache. This solution ensures that a task is *only* performed *once* for a given key. This mechanism is also very useful for keeping tracking of Deferred Objects for given requests for debugging and logging purposes.

怪士 Karura

Figure 5-5. Karura framework

Karura Framework

The Karura is a divine creature with human torso and birdlike head in Japanese Hindu-Buddhist mythology.

— Wikipedia

As part of this book, we are also introducing Karura (shown in Figure 5-5), a lightweight web application framework we have developed for building hybrid applications. Karura features a custom message dispatcher module for routing methods from Java to JavaScript.

We do this by associating each JavaScript object with a callback handle implicitly. This callback handle is automatically made available to the Java objects, and is then used for routing the responses back to JavaScript.

For more details on this approach, you can look at *karura.js* for JavaScript and the WebView Plug-in for Java dispatch framework respectively.

Karura is different from PhoneGap (*http://goo.gl/FMpTe*), Cordova (*http://goo.gl/nbdst*), and other web application frameworks in the sense that it leverages autogeneration to generate JavaScript for components that have been exposed through the WebView. This allows developers to concentrate on application logic without requiring them to write thousands of lines of JavaScript code to access the native components.

Hence, the Karura framework has been named after this hybrid creature based on the story in Japanese Hindu-Buddhist mythology. Karura framework is distributed under GPL and Commercial Licenses.

Karura framework can be found at GitHub (*https://github.com/karuradev*).

Thread Safety

When accessing Java objects from the JavaScript layer, the methods may be accessed from a private, background thread associated with the WebView that is different than the main application/UI thread that the Java layer typically runs in.

This means that application developers need to be cautious of thread safety while accessing the exposed Java functions and the object's fields directly from those functions.

Our recommended approach for solving this problem would be to use the functions exposed to the JavaScript layer to queue the requests using a handler associated with a main thread. The handler can then dispatch these events on the main thread, thereby taking care of any threading issues.

You can extend this concept further by queuing non-UI related events on the non-UI loopers (and associated handlers). This will allow you to keep your UI thread lightweight and responsive.

## CHAPTER 6

HTML Architecture for Hybrid Applications

Your hybrid application is primarily an HTML5 web page built using mobile-optimized JavaScript and CSS-styled to look and feel native. Like any application, hybrid applications can be rather complex depending upon the user experience. For the sake of simplicity, let's assume a simple app that contains a single WebView and a single entry point web page—for example, *index.html*. An hybrid application will be visible to users like any other application on the application launcher. Once users tap on the application launch icon, the main activity will be created containing a WebView with no browser chrome visible. Upon creation, the WebView will load your default entry point web page to initiate the user experience. From that point on, the design of the web component is completely your choice, however single page applications have recently emerged as a de facto design strategy for these applications. Let's look at this design pattern in slightly more detail.

Architecture of a Web Application

A typical web application can architecturally be represented as shown in Figure 6-1.

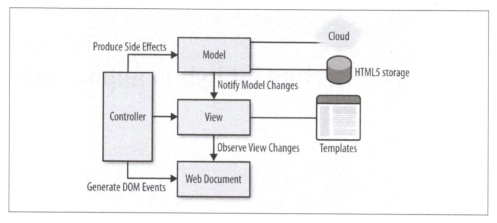

Figure 6-1. Web Application Architecture

The architecture is self explanatory, however, we would like to reiterate a few salient points:

- UI events generate DOM objects based on user interactions.
- The model abstracts network connectivity and storage making the controller and views agnostic of the source and destination for data.
- The model is assumed to be the only component that stores anything about the data.

Single Page Applications (SPA)

A *single page application* is a web application in which the entire user experience is contained within a single web page. SPA architecture empowers mobile web applications to become more uniform. These apps persistently run the same page with different views or content, but without reloading or navigating away to another resource. This is achieved by separating the data from the presentation layer and relies heavily on Java-Script.

SPA architecture uses the fragment identifier, which is introduced by a hashtag (#) in the URL location, followed by an anchor identifier to point to an element in the HTML document. For example, if your website URL looks like this *http://oreilly.com/index.html#article*, The fragment `article` refers to an HTML element with an `id="article"` attribute in the *index.html* document.

One caveat, though, is that this technique can break the browser's page history navigation so that it will not allow you to hit the Back/Forward buttons to navigate the resources. Using JavaScript, we could take advantage of this particular functionality to navigate our views within the same HTML document without changing the current state of the document. There are many JavaScript libraries that rely on this simple technique in order to build an MVC pattern for web applications. Particularly, using this pattern may improve the user experience in the mobile web applications with limited resources. We will be using `Backbone.js` to leverage SPA experiences in our sample application.

Key Design Considerations for Single Page Applications

Here are some things to keep in mind when creating single-page applications:

- Modularize your code as much as possible.
- Try to make these modules independent of each other, if possible.
- Use the proper access paradigm for variable names. Make sure you do not expose what is not required.
- Develop a mechanism wherein you can explicitly identify module dependencies and hence load them at runtime.
- Additionally, it would be beneficial if non-UI modules can be run from the command line. This will greatly facilitate unit testing.

The Libraries and Frameworks for Your Hybrid Apps

You can find many different JavaScript libraries tailored for mobile applications. It is ultimately your choice to pick ones that are suitable for your needs. If you are using open source software, ensure that the software license is aligned with your company's third-party software policies. We prefer the following libraries and frameworks for flexibility and licensing.

Backbone.js for MVC Framework

`Backbone.js` helps us organize our code into manageable sections, namely models, collections, and views. It is a lightweight library that provides structure to single-page applications using a hashtag and exclamation mark (#!) together in the URL location for its routing (HTML5 `pushstate` is also available). It uses JSON format for its models and collections excessively without tying the data to the DOM. One of the most useful features is that the models in collections can be bound to UI views (HTML) and automatically updated as data changes.

`Backbone.js` has become a very popular JavaScript framework for web and mobile applications. You can download this library from the Backbone website (*http://goo.gl/ Ez60R*).

Underscore.js for Utility Support

Underscore.js is a utility-belt library for JavaScript that provides support for the usual functional suspects (each, map, reduce, filter…) without extending any core JavaScript objects. Additionally Underscore.js has a powerful feature that can compile JavaScript templates into functions that can be evaluated for rendering. While there are many JavaScript templating engines available, we will use Underscore.js for our sample project, because we will be using Backbone.js, which requires Underscore.js as its only hard requirement anyway. The Underscore.js library also offers 80-odd handy functions that enhance Backbone.js.

You can download this library and access documentation from Underscore website (*http://goo.gl/5YsWY*).

iScroll.js for scrolling

iScroll.js is a must-have library that enables scrolling the view using JavaScript. This library was developed to accommodate the limitations of the mobile WebKit, which does not provide a native and cross-device way to scroll content inside a fixed width/ height element.

You can obtain the iScroll library from the iScroll 4 website (*http://goo.gl/fsLGK*). You may also follow the iScroll 5 beta group at the iScroll 5 group website (*http://goo.gl/ jddTY*). To use iScroll.js, list items need to be appended to an iScroll container element.

```
<div id="wrapper">
    <div id="scroller">
        <ul id="thelist">
                        <li>row 1</li>
                        <li>row 2</li>
                        <li>row 3</li>
                        <li>row 4</li>
                </ul>
        </div>
</div>
var myScroll = new iScroll('wrapper');
```

iScroll Caveats

Since a list needs to be prepopulated, you may experience performance issues when you render a large amount of list items, such as 1,000 rows in a roster. Of course, you can use pagination to break down the content into multiple views, however, there are cases where you want to list all of your content within the same view.

Ideally, `iScroll` should allow us to append items to the DOM progressively as you scroll, which is currently not supported. One approach to overcome this limitation would be to progressively load the content into scrolling area using `setTimeout(func, delay)`. This way we can load an initial set of items into the view to give the illusion that the content is loaded fast enough to view, thereafter, we can append the rest of the elements to the scrolling container as the user starts scrolling.

This method works fine for a relatively small list of items in the list view. The ideal solution would be appending the list items to the scrolling view one by one dynamically as you scroll. This optimization technique would offer a better user experience than the previous one we mentioned here.

jQuery.js for JavaScript application

`jQuery.js` has become the industry standard JavaScript library for building interactive client-side applications. It provides many APIs that can handle the quirks between different browsers implementations of the core JavaScript functions. It also features a fast *chainable* API framework. One can argue that writing native functions can run faster than jQuery, which encapsulates them, and while this can be true, writing maintainable code and overcoming the cross-browser issues is primarily our focus. We also find jQuery fast enough that it does not pose a problem with mobile performance, especially considering it is loaded directly from the device.

Preload Images Within the CSS Files

For our sample application, we will be using a jQuery plug-in to preload the images in our CSS documents. The `preloadCssImages.jQuery_v5.js` plug-in offers an unobtrusive way to preload all your images from different directories, which are defined in your CSS files.

You can download this library from the jQuery-Preload-CSS-Images plug-in website (*http://goo.gl/Gj6Eh*).

```
$(document).ready(function(){
        $.preloadCssImages();
});
```

 At the time of this writing, we have observed that the images that are defined in the CSS documents are not loaded properly in the Web-View UI by Android. This could happen for several reasons. Using `preloadCssImages.jQuery_v5.js`, you can work around these issues by downloading images explicitly.

CSS Reset Avoids Browser Inconsistencies

Not all browsers are created equal, the same goes for mobile browsers. CSS Reset is a way to keep the rendering results as universal as possible by resetting the built-in default style values to a baseline value before your custom CSS is applied.

HTML5 Boilerplate provides two CSS files (*main.css* and *normalize.css*), which offers a nice way of resetting your browser's default style settings. You can download these files from the Html5boilerplate website (*http://goo.gl/3JUxZ*).

```
/*
Sample CSS Reset
*/
html, body, div, form, fieldset, legend, label {
        margin: 0;
        padding: 0;
        border: 0px;
        outline: 0px;
        font-size: 100%;
}
```

Your Home index.html

The *index.html* web page will be launched by the WebView when an activity starts. This web page is normally placed in the *assets* directory. We defined the `viewport` meta tag, which controls the initial appearance when the web page loads. The CSS `link` tag was intentionally left blank because we like to load our CSS files using JavaScript by respecting the `window.devicePixelRatio` window property.

 We discovered that in some older versions of the Android API, our sample app was crashing when processing the **0.75** Device Pixel Ratio (DPR) while loading the CSS using the `link` tag. We were able to re-produce this abnormal crash with a few more same-generation phones as well. However, the usage that follows is more responsive than loading these CSS files in JavaScript; you may see a nonstyled view first for a split second, then a styled version will be shown due to the `onDomReady()` delay in JavaScript.

The following way of loading your CSS into the DOM is the ideal way:

```
<link rel="stylesheet"
        media="screen and (-webkit-min-device-pixel-ratio: 0.75)"
        href="ldpi.css" />
<link rel="stylesheet"
        media="screen and (-webkit-min-device-pixel-ratio: 1.0)"
        href="mdpi.css" />
<link rel="stylesheet"
```

```
           media="screen and (-webkit-min-device-pixel-ratio: 1.5)"
           href="hdpi.css" />
<link rel="stylesheet"
           media="screen and (-webkit-min-device-pixel-ratio: 2.0)"
           href="xhdpi.css" />
```

Other possible solutions follow, but are not recommended unless it is necessary to load your CSS this way.

Loading CSS using a JavaScript function for different DPIs:

```
function loadCSS() {
        switch(window.devicePixelRatio) {
                case 2.0:
                        $('#dpr-css').attr('href', 'css/xhdpi.css'); ❶
                        break;
                case 1.5:
                        $('#dpr-css').attr('href', 'css/hdpi.css');
                        break;
                case 0.75:
                        $('#dpr-css').attr('href', 'css/ldpi.css');
                        break;
                default: // 1
                        $('#dpr-css').attr('href', 'css/mdpi.css');
        }
}
```

❶   #dpr-css is the ID of your stylesheet <link> tag in the HTML.

```
<link id="dpr-css" rel="stylesheet"
      href="css/default.css"
      type="text/css"
      media="screen" />
```

Alternatively, you can append your stylesheets to the DOM for different densities using the following code. However, we do not recommend this technique.

```
$('HEAD').append($('<link rel="stylesheet" href="xhdpi.css" type="text/css"
      media="screen and (-webkit-min-device-pixel-ratio: 2.0)" />'));
```

Here's a sample source of a template file for a hybrid Android application:

```
<script type="text/x-tmpl" id="tmpl_contacts_item">
<div class="contact item" data-id="<%= id %>">
        <div class="edit">Edit</div>
    <div class="profile">
        <img data-id="<%= id %>" class="avatar" src="<%= avatar %>" />
          <div class="full_name"><%= name.givenName %> <%= name.familyName %></
div>
    </div>
    <% if (emails.length > 0) { %>
    <div class="details">
        <div class="caption emails">Emails</div>
        <% _.each(emails, function(email) { %>
```

```
                <div class="comm"><span><%= email.type %></span> :
                <a href="mailto:<%= email.value %>"><%= email.value %></a></div>
                <% }); %>
        </div>
        <% } %>
        <% if (phoneNumbers.length > 0) { %>
        <div class="details">
            <div class="caption phones">Phones</div>
                <% _.each(phoneNumbers, function(phone) { %>
                <div class="comm"><span><%= phone.type %></span> :
                <a href="tel:<%= phone.value %>"><%= phone.value %></a></div>
                <% }); %>
        </div>
        <% } %>
        <% if (note != '') { %>
        <div class="details">
            <div class="caption notes">Notes</div>
            <div class="note"><%= note %></div>
        </div>
        <% } %>
    </div>
    </script>
```

Viewport Meta Tag

The viewport meta tag defines a set of properties that describes the behavior and initial appearance of the web page when it is rendered for the first time based on the device screen size. The *viewport* is the section of the web page that is shown in the view. This viewport meta tag is supported by many mobile browsers.

Viewport Width

The width of the viewport in pixels tells the browser how best to render the web page width-wise. In this example, we are targeting 320 px wide screens to display our content.

```
<meta name="viewport" content="width=320">
```

This does not scale the view for different screen sizes. In particular, Android device fragmentation makes this more of a concern than on other platforms. So using the device-width value for the width property in the viewport tag would allow the content to be scaled to the available width on the screen.

```
<meta name="viewport" content="width=device-width">
```

In this case, whether your screen width is 480 px in portrait mode or 800 px in landscape mode, the device-width value makes the available width independent of how wide your screen is.

Viewport Scaling with the Content Attribute

Here are a few of the available options for the `content` attribute:

`initial-scale`

> The initial zoom of a web page. Its scale is a multiplier from 0 to 10.0 that sets the scale of a web page after its first display. The larger value zooms in, but 1.0 means no zoom.

`minimum-scale`

> The minimum multiplier the user is able to zoom out of a web page. 1.0 does not allow any zooms. Its scale is from 0 to 10.0.

`maximum-scale`

> The maximum multiplier the user is able to zoom in to a web page. 1.0 does not allow any zooms. Its scale is from 0 to 10.0.

`user-scalable`

> The permission (yes/no) as to whether the user is able to control the scale (zoom in/out) of the web page or not. The default value is yes.

Support for the `target-densitydpi=device-dpi` property has been dropped from WebKit in favor of responsive images and CSS device units. This property was not supported by iOS anyway. The issue can be followed at the WebKit bug website (*http://goo.gl/URmQd*).

```
<meta name="viewport" content="width=device-width,
      minimum-scale=1,
      initial-scale=1,
      maximum-scale=1,
      user-scalable=no" />
```

This meta tag has an important role when optimizing the web page for mobile devices. It basically prevents the mobile browsers from altering the zoom level of that web page unilaterally.

Responsive Design and Media Queries

In the mobile app paradigm, responsive design should be carefully considered when it comes to content adaptation and presentation because the available screen area is limited.

Media queries in CSS3 help the application adapt to different sets of properties and rules for your CSS styling. Media queries allow us to target not only certain generations of devices but also to scrutinize some of the characteristics of a device to target certain styling attributes such as `orientation`, `device-aspect-ratio`, `color`, or `resolution`.

Responsive design is fulfilled by using the media queries in the CSS files to improve the *device-specific* response while the `media` attribute controls which styles to apply.

There are three ways to define CSS media queries in your HTML documents. We will be using the first technique in our sample application.

In the `<style>` element as media rules:

```
<style type="text/css">
        @media only screen and (-webkit-min-device-pixel-ratio: 1.0) {
                /* some CSS definitions here */
        }
        @media only screen and (orientation: portrait){
                /* some CSS definitions here */
        }
        @media only screen and (orientation: landscape){
                /* some CSS definitions here */
        }
</style>
```

As an external include:

```
<link rel="stylesheet"
        type="text/css" href="small_screen.css"
        media="only screen and (max-width: 320px)" />
```

by importing the stylesheet:

```
@import "small_screen.css" only screen and (max-width: 320px);
```

Android provides WebKit as a rendering engine, which supports a proprietary property called `-webkit-min-device-pixel-ratio` that returns the pixel density of that device. There are currently at least four possible values for the Device Pixel Ratio (DPR): `0.75`, `1.0`, `1.5`, and `2.0`. These values can accessed from JavaScript using the `window.device PixelRatio` window property.

- If the DPR is 0.75, the device is considered low density and the web page is scaled down by default.

- If the DPR is 1, the device is considered medium density and the web page is not scaled at all.

- If the DPR is 1.5, the device is considered high density and the web page is scaled up by this ratio.

- If the DPR is 2, the device is considered extra high density and the web page is scaled up by this ratio.

To understand a little bit more about pixel density, see this in-depth article by Peter-Paul Koch, visit the Quirksmode website (*http://goo.gl/hKYlS*) for pixel density.

EM or Percent (%) unit for scalable interface

There are several kinds of units available for scaling an HTML element in the browser: EMs (em), Root Ems (rem), Pixels (px), Picas (pc), Exes (ex), Percents (%), and Points (pt). However, some of them are not largely supported for the font-size property to scale the text size in the CSS document.

We focus on two of these for mobile applications: em and %. If you would like to display the correct size of text in all screen resolutions, em or % is the ideal solution because they are the most commonly used ones for the font sizes on the Web, but which one is more preferable and why? Designers and developers are often confused with which to choose for font size in the CSS properties.

Normally, the WebKit renders the font sizes as 16 px (16 sp in Android) unless you change the default font size in the WebKit settings explicitly using the setDefaultFont Size() method. In other words, most web browser render the font sizes as the 16px, which is equal to 1em or 100%. However, we do not recommend you use the px unit for the font sizes in your CSS documents.

The W3C also recommends using em or % for the font sizes for more scalable and robust stylesheets. We actually found out that using percent (%) for the font size allows designers to preserve readability for maximum consistency and accessibility in visual designs.

 Sometimes setting a font-size value to an inner HTML tag may not give you the result that you expect. This is because the inner element inherits the font-size from its parent and applies its own font-size relative to its parent's font-size. As a result, you may end up seeing a smaller font.

Font size inheritance in nested HTML tags looks like the following:

```
header {
    font-size: 2em;
        /*font-size: 200%;*/
}
span {
    font-size: 0.5em;
        /*font-size: 50%;*/
}
<header>This is a large header without any nested tag</header>
<header>This is a large header with <span>a span tag</span></header>
<span>This is a span tag</span>
```

Therefore, the first <header> tag has a font size as 2em, which is twice the base font size, then the inner <span> tag in the second <header> tag will inherit its parent tag as 2em, then it will multiple with 0.5. It will result in 1em, but if you look at the second <span>

tag, its font size is actually the correct 0.5em. Both em and % units get bigger as the base font size increases. The font experiment can be seen at the Jsfiddle website (*http://goo.gl/AVRxh*).

It is also possible that you may need to convert px to em or vice versa. You may programmatically do the conversions using this handy jQuery plug-in in your application. Visit the jQuery-Pixel-Em-Converter plug-in website (*http://goo.gl/BwjJZ*) or use the tool at the Pxtoem website (*http://goo.gl/iTYJE*).

CSS3 Introduces rem Unit

The rem unit is relative to the root (<html>) element. You can define a root font size, and then you can use that font size as a baseline within your CSS document. As we mentioned earlier, em causes a compounding issue for nested elements, which inherit the font-size from their parents, whereas the rem unit prevents this undesired behavior and gives designers and developers control of the font size by taking the percentage of the root (<html>) element's font size for each element independently, even if they are nested.

Opacity or RGBA: What Is the Difference?

The opacity property in CSS specifies the amount of transparency for an element. Its value can be anywhere from 0.0 to 1. A lower opacity value means the element can be more transparent. A higher value means the element is fully opaque. The main difference between opacity and RGBA is that opacity affects an element's children with the same opacity level while RGBA has an effect on the transparency of a single element only for independent opacity.

```
-webkit-opacity: 0.5;
```

RGBA stands for *Red, Green, Blue, and Alpha*. CSS3 introduced the RGBA support to set the alpha transparency, which sets the opacity via the alpha channel and controls how much of what is behind the color shows through.

```
background: rgba(255, 0, 0, 0.5);
```

WebKit supports RGBA in CSS properties; however, there is a performance issue with RGBA in scrolling views. We will talk about these performance tips and tricks in later chapters.

We will use the RGBA conversion tool at Devoth's HEX 2 RGBA Color Calculator website (*http://goo.gl/R7X82*) to convert HEX colors to RGBA format for our example application.

Event Pooling

As your application gets complex, managing events can be burdensome. Organizing the events into an event pooling mechanism, which is a variation of observer pattern, mechanism might be one alternative solution to manage dependencies. jQuery offers the `bind` and the `trigger` APIs to handle event pooling in a easy way. Event pooling can be really useful when the events are dispatched from the Java layer using Android Web-View.

Here is an example of event pooling using jQuery's `bind` and the `trigger` APIs.

```
function updateContact(e, data) {
        switch(e.type) {
                case 'NAME_UPDATE':
                        // update the name
                        // data.name
                        break;
                case 'PHONE_UPDATE':
                        // update the phone number
                        // data.phone_number
                        break;
                default:
                        // default action
        }
}
```

The following code allows us to bind an event to the document, which can be then called from various sources, such as HTML, a URL location, or JavaScript code itself using the `trigger` API in jQuery. You may notice that multiple event names can be registered using the `bind` API.

```
function subscribeEvents(eventName, callback) {
        $(document).bind(eventName, callback);
}

subscribeEvents('NAME_UPDATE PHONE_UPDATE', function(e, data) {
        updateContact.apply(null, [e, data]);
});
```

Using the following code, we can easily encapsulate a common functionality into the `triggerEvent()` method in which triggering an event would be very easy using the `eventName`, `args`, and `delay` parameters.

```
function triggerEvent(eventName, args, delay) {
        setTimeout(function() {
                $(document).trigger(eventName, args);
        }, delay || 0);
}
```

Once you subscribe to your events using subscribeEvents() function, you can trigger these events from HTML, using the URL location from the Android WebView or you call them from the JavaScript code itself.

```
// from HTML
<input type="text" name="full_name"
    onKeyUp="triggerEvent('NAME_UPDATE',  {  name  :  $(this).val().trim()  },
100);" />

// from URL location (Android WebView can trigger this)
JavaScript: triggerEvent('NAME_UPDATE', { name : 'Karura' }, 100)

// or from JavaScript code
triggerEvent('NAME_UPDATE', { name : 'Karura' }, 100);
```

 For some reason, when Android WebView executes the JavaScript: func(); code in the URL location, the WebView gains the focus and dismisses the soft keyboard while typing in a form field. This behavior can cause very unpleasant experiences for users if they are chatting in your app. One ideal solution could be that when a user focuses into a form field, you either detect the focus in the Java layer or notify the Java layer from JavaScript, then pull the content and events using JavaScript from the Java layer. By doing so, you can prevent the Android WebView from gaining focus while dispatching the events to the UI layer.

## CHAPTER 7

CSS, DOM, and JavaScript: Optimization Tips and Useful Snippets

In this chapter, we will explore how to build snappy mobile applications by taking advantage of high-performance optimization techniques while avoiding memory leaks. Performance is a big focus for mobile applications, as smartphones have limited resources.

Image garbage collection

The images in the view may not be immediately garbage collected when you remove the DOM container element. In order to release the previous image reference, you can assign a 1x1 pixel transparent data image src attribute before safely removing the image object. You can encode this image as base64 to avoid a network request.

```
function removeImage(image) {
        image.src = 'data:image/gif;base64,R0lGODlhAQABAAD/ACwAAAAAAQABAAA-
CADs=';
        setTimeout(function () {
                delete image.src;
                image = null;
        }, 0);
}
```

Data URI images

Use of base64 encoded data images is very popular in mobile apps. It involves inlining your image data straight into the HTML or CSS page. It allows images to load instantly with your web app's HTML page—something very important if you want your app to function like a native app. An additional benefit is that you can easily retrieve relatively small images like the avatars within the JSON strings from the Java layer. If you want to create data URI images manually, you can use the following command in your terminal window:

```
openssl base64 -in image.png
```

Preloading images

Perhaps some of your web data needs to come from a dynamic remote resource or is too large to use base64. You can also preload images to cache in your app browser's memory. This solution is perfect for login pages or other "doorways" where you have the opportunity to load data in the background.

```
function loadImage(src) {
        var image = new Image();
        image.src = src;
        image.onerror = function() {
                debug.error('Missing image source: ' + this.src);
        };
        return image;
}

var image = loadImage('path/to/image');
image.onload = function() {
        // do something
};
```

Avoid using `text-shadow`, `box-shadow`, `border-radius`, `gradient`, `opacity`, *CSS RGBA, and image transparency*

These styling effects can slow down the scrolling in the WebKit. The issues with `text-shadow` and `box-shadow` are already resolved in the current WebKit, but the Android version of WebKit hasn't been fixed yet. So, use them on scrolling areas sparingly; visit the WebKit bug website (*http://goo.gl/SJf87*) for additional information. Also, using the `opacity` and CSS RGBA properties in CSS may interfere with hardware accelerated rendering in the scroll view. If these effects are needed, use lightweight *.png* graphics that combine many of these effects into one static image or experiment with how much you can do in CSS3 and how much you will need to statically create. This is especially required for scrolling or animating areas of your application.

Use CSS3 Transitions instead of JavaScript animations

CSS3 Transitions are hardware accelerated, harnessing not just the CPU but the GPU of the video card. They offer much smoother user experiences than their counterpart.

```
-webkit-transition: width 1s;
```

Image sprites

An image sprite is a collection of images placed into a single image while assigning a unique position for each one. Using image sprites will reduce the number of HTTP requests to the web server and save bandwidth. It is also an ideal technique for game applications in order to load images faster. For example, you could put all the world countries' flags in a single CSS sprite. This concept can be easily used in the Android

Java layer as well. You can find more about this example at the Flag-sprites website (*http://goo.gl/NWStf*).

Object caching
Caching the JavaScript and DOM variables allows you to access them faster in the iterations or later in the code.

```
var $box = $('#box'), len = $box.length;
for(var i=0; i < len; i++) {
        $box[i].show();
}
```

Use more specific DOM selectors
Using more specific DOM selectors can speed up your application, as there are fewer elements that JavaScript needs to iterate through.

```
$('input.username') selector is faster than $('.username')
input[type="..."] selector is faster than [type="..."]
```

Avoid multiple reflows using DocumentFragment
The `DocumentFragment` object allows us to reduce DOM manipulations while we can insert multiple HTML elements outside of the DOM without reflowing. Once you move these elements from a temporary location to the DOM in a single operation, the `DocumentFragment` triggers a single reflow, which is a real booster.

```
var fragment = document.createDocumentFragment();
```

Use Web Workers to compute heavy processing
Web Workers can improve your application responsiveness and performance while doing CPU intensive tasks in background threads. Be aware that Web Workers cannot access the DOM layer.

```
// non-ui.js
self.onmessage = function(event) {
        self.postMessage(event.data);
}

var worker = new Worker('non-ui.js');
worker.onmessage = function(event){
        console.log('result: ' + event.data);
}
worker.postMessage("O'Reilly books");
```

translate3d(0, 0, 0) is hardware accelerated
Using `translate3d` on elements can activate the GPU for compositing and optimizing the performance for animations. It can make a complex animation that is a little jerky silky smooth. Be careful, however, as overusing this trick can lead to poor battery performance.

```
-webkit-transform: translate3d(0, 0, 0);
```

Use event delegation

Having a lot of event listeners in your code can reduce the performance and its responsiveness. When you can attach an event listener to the parent element, event delegation can handle all the events for its children in the event bubbling phase.

Caching the style object

Caching the `style` object into a variable improves the performance of UI repaint or redraw.

```
// 1
var element = document.getElementById('id');
element.style.backgroundColor = 'red';

// 2 - this is faster
var style = document.getElementById('id').style;
style.backgroundColor = 'red';
```

setTimeout(fn, 0) is helpful

The JavaScript runs on a single thread, which is called the UI thread in a single window context. When using the `setTimeout()` with 0 delay, it allows the JavaScript interpreter to finish the current call stack, and creates a new call stack to be added to the *event queue* on the nearest timer tick. It also eludes seeing the "Script is running too long" warning message. This is helpful in many situations, for example, if you need to manipulate a DOM element and then right after access it. Adding the `setTimeout()` optimization guarantees the DOM modification is done before the element is ready to be accessed.

requestAnimationFrame() is for animations

Avoid using times or intervals for your animation in JavaScript. The `requestAnimationFrame()` or `rAF` allows the browser to run smoother animations with higher frames per second and higher timer precision in an efficient way.

Detecting devices

When it comes to content adaptation and ironing out platform differences, detecting the device platform would be handy. Use the following code snippets to identify the current device:

```
var devices = {
        isMobile : (navigator.userAgent.indexOf('Mobile') > -1),
        isAndroid : (/android/gi).test(navigator.appVersion),
        isIDevice : (/iPhone|iPad//iPod/gi).test(navigator.appVersion)
}
```

Detecting touch events

This simple touch event detection snippet can identify whether the device supports touch events or not, and it falls back to desktop click events if not supported.

```
var isTouch = !!('ontouchstart' in window);
var touchEvents = {
```

```
          CANCEL : (window.ontouchcancel !== undefined ?
                              'touchcancel' : 'mouseup'),
          START  : (window.ontouchstart !== undefined ?
                              'touchstart' : 'mousedown'),
          MOVE   : (window.ontouchmove !== undefined ?
                              'touchmove' : 'mousemove'),
          END    : (window.ontouchend !== undefined ?
                              'touchend' : 'mouseup')

// usage 1
$('BODY').bind(touchEvents.START, function() {
        // do something
});

// usage 2
$(document).on(touchEvents.START + ' ' + touchEvents.END,
                        '.inactive',
                        function() {
                                $(this).toggleClass('active');
                        });
```

Removing the address bar

If you are building a hybrid app using Android WebView, no need to worry about this, however, if you are building a mobile web app, then you may consider the following code to remove the address bar from the browser:

```
$(window).bind('load', function() {
        setTimeout(function() {
                window.scrollTo(0, 1);
        }, 0);
});
```

Preventing page bouncing

When you drag the top of the page down, it will partially scroll vertically. When you release your finger it will bounce back to its original position. This behavior is often undesired; you can disable it using this snippet:

```
$(document).bind(touchEvents.MOVE, function(e) {
        e.preventDefault();
});
```

Detecting orientation change

This code registers the orientationchange event to the window object and allows you to access the four different orientation states:

```
$(window).bind('orientationchange', function() {
        switch (window.orientation) {
                case 0:
                        // portrait (normal)
                        break;
                case 180:
                        // portrait (upside-down)
```

```
                    break;
            case -90:
                    // landscape (clockwise)
                    break;
            case 90:
                    // landscape (counter-clockwise)
                    break;
            default:
                    //
    }
});
```

Detecting resize change

This code registers the resize event to the window object and allows you to access the resize event. One caveat is that when orientation occurs, both orientation and resize events are fired.

```
var heightBefore = $('body').css('height');
$(window).bind('resize', function() {
        var heightAfter = $('body').css('height');
        console.info('onResize: ' + heightBefore + '-' + heightAfter);
});
```

## CHAPTER 8

Publishing Apps for Android

The application development lifecycle can be thought of as an iterative process involving design, development, distribution, monitoring of user response, bug fixes, and enhancements. This chapter aims at describing the process involved for making your application available for users to download and install on their devices. An optimum distribution and discovery infrastructure plays a key role in making sure your application will be found among millions of other apps and will be employed by users on an ongoing basis.

Applications are distributed through well known discovery and distribution channels, often known as market places. There are a number of distribution channels available to Android applications developers including ones from Google Play (*http://goo.gl/BdmoS*), Amazon (*http://goo.gl/RtT2x*), and GetJar (*http://goo.gl/ro02u*). These marketplaces allow users to discover, download, and pay for applications.

The process of distributing your applications across various market places is quite similar in principle, however, the modalities may differ. From 30,000 feet, the publication workflow can be summarized as a sequence of the following steps:

1. Register a publisher/developer account.
2. Set up the merchant account for payments.
3. Upload the marketing material for your application.
4. Determine whether you would like to run alpha and beta programs for your application.
5. Decide the price for your application, if you wish to charge for it.
6. Digitally sign your application.
7. Upload the application.

8. Wait for approval, if any. If your application is rejected during this phase, incorporate comments and resubmit the application.

9. Wait for your application to go live.

 Some of these steps might be optional or may need to be performed only once per developer.

Even though most of the marketplaces are for discovery and distribution of content including Android applications, almost all of them also offer tools and services to developers to track the performance of their application through usage analytics and detailed crash logs. We will also look at some of these features as we sail along in this chapter.

From the end consumer perspective, these marketplaces can be accessed from both the device or the desktop. Hence, you must prepare and upload marketing material that suits multiple form factors.

 In this chapter, we will look at the application publication process for Google Play (*http://goo.gl/BdmoS*) and Amazon App Store (*http://goo.gl/RtT2x*) in detail, however, process for Samsung, GetJar, and SlideMe are quite similar.

The application publication process should not be undermined in any way. This process should typically start around the same time as the application features and business model definition phase. This is important because some of the publication-related decisions will affect the design of your application as well. Things you may want to consider for publication include:

1. The marketplaces in which you wish to make your application available. This is because different app stores might have different in-app purchase or license verification libraries, which you may have to incorporate in your applications based on your choice of these marketplaces.

2. Whether you would like to charge for your application.

3. If you would like to have a beta program for your application.

4. If you would like to have different free and paid versions of the app.

5. Features in free and paid versions of the application.

6. If you would like to offer your application using a subscription model.

7. Are their any specific devices that need to be targeted for your applications. This may seem to be unnecessarily short-sighted at first because obviously you would want your application to be available on as many devices as possible. However, please bear in mind that some app stores like Amazon, Samsung, and BlackBerry are device specific and if you are targeting these app stores, then you may have to cater to certain device profiles or ensure that certain marketplace requirements are adhered to by the applications.

As part of the application release (publication) process, you may additionally want to:

1. Test your application across multiple devices, screen form factors, and orientations.

2. Verify that your application meets the guidelines put forth by the respective app store content guidelines.

3. Turn off all debugging diagnostics for release, including any extraneous logging that could affect application performance.

4. Verify that the debuggable option is off.

5. Run stability testing on your application using tools like *monkeyrunner* and *monkey*.

6. Replace all debug API keys with the release versions (you can also achieve this by either using a factory pattern driven off the `BuildConfig` class or using a dedicated configuration for release).

7. Take your application through PEN(etration) testing if you provide access to critical information through your app.

8. Prepare your *AndroidManifest.xml* file by:

    a. Minimizing the permissions set by removing unused permissions.

    b. Verify that the application icon (various sizes of PNG) is set appropriately.

    c. Verify that the application label is set appropriately.

    d. Verify that the application version name is set appropriately.

    e. Verify that the application version code is set appropriately. The version code is a number that the Android platform uses to manage application upgrades.

    f. Make sure you have the appropriate `uses-feature` tag in the file to allow Google Play to filter your application for the right set of devices.

    g. Make sure only valid sets of activities are exported by the application.

    h. Internationalize your app, based on the markets you wish to release the application on. This can include the following:

        i. Text Strings

        ii. Icons and images

        iii. Colors

iv. Some layouts (if needed)

v. Marketing material and screenshots

9. Obfuscate and optimize code.

If your application requires certain capabilities from the device, you can use the `uses-feature` tag in *AndroidManifest.xml*. This information is used by the Android platform as a hint to determine the compatibility of the device with your app. However, it is always a good practice to have a fallback behavior in your application if a particular capability is not present.

This can be achieve by the setting the required param in the tag to `false`, for example:

```
<uses-feature android:name="android.hardware.bluetooth"
        android:required="false" />
```

This will allow the Google Play to show that Bluetooth is required for the application to run but is not mandatory. You can then adapt the user experience by checking the availability of Bluetooth on the device at runtime by querying the `PackageManager` service as follows:

```
boolean hasBluetooth =
        getPackageManager().hasSystemFeature(PackageManager.FEATURE_BLUETOOTH);
```

Depending upon the value of `hasBluetooth`, you can adapt the user experience of the application in accordance with device capability. One example would be to not show a Bluetooth headset option in VoIP clients on devices that do not have a Bluetooth radio available.

Digitally Signing Applications

Android application packages must be digitally signed for the Android package manager to install them. To do this, you must generate a private key. A private key identifies the developer and is critical to building trust relationships. It is very important to secure the private key information.

The private key can be used to digitally sign the release package files of your Android application, as well as any upgrades. Application updates must be signed with the same private key. For security reasons, the Android package manager does not install the update over the existing application if the key is different. This means you need to keep the key corresponding with the application in a secure, easy-to-find location for future use.

Android, like other Java platforms, follows the self-sign model for applications. This means there is no certification authority to validate your authority, but the Android package manager can ensure that subsequent updates for the app are from the same developer. Also, as your application becomes bigger and more successful, it will end up establishing a sort of identity for you as a developer users can trust. Details on digitally signing your applications can be found at the Signing Your Applications website (*http:// goo.gl/eccZB*).

Protecting Your Application with ProGuard

The Android toolchain includes built-in support for the ProGuard tool to help you secure your application.

Some ProGuard benefits include:

- Shrinking code
- Optimizing
- Remove dead code
- Obfuscating the source code

Enabling ProGuard is simple; there is a *proguard-project.txt* configuration file associated with your application project. You can add, delete, and customize `proguard` rules in this file. Once `proguard` rules have been specified, you can then update the `proguard.con fig` setting within the application's *project.properties* configuration file to point at the ProGuard configuration file, like this:

```
proguard.config=proguard-project.txt
```

For more information on using ProGuard, see its documentation at the Android developer ProGuard website (*http://goo.gl/w66Ku*).

Google Play

Play is a digital distribution platform from Google, where you can buy Android applications among other media (for example, books, video, and audio). The Play store is the default application marketplace installed on a Google Certified Android device, although you may use additional stores as well, depending upon the service provider and the device manufacturer.

Registering as a Publisher

Before you can publish apps on Google Play, you need to register a developer account. Registering the developer account is simple process and can be initiated at the Google Play website (*http://goo.gl/YjCzV*). To publish applications on Google Play you will need a Google account. Follow the URL and sign in with your Google account, as shown in Figure 8-1.

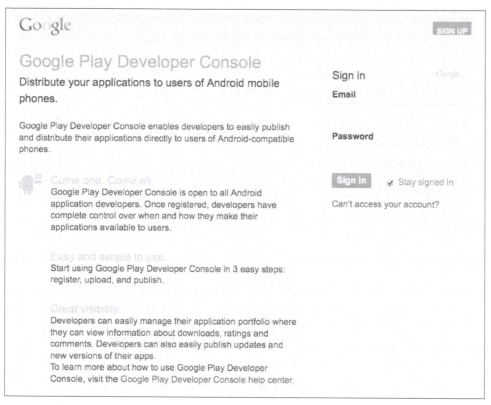

Figure 8-1. Sign into Google Play

If you do not have an account, then you can create one by clicking on the Sign Up button, shown in Figure 8-2.

As part of the sign up process, you will be asked to provide your contact details and an email address along with some personal information. The personal information, such as phone number and date of birth, are used to allow you to unlock your account in the future in case you forget your sign in information.

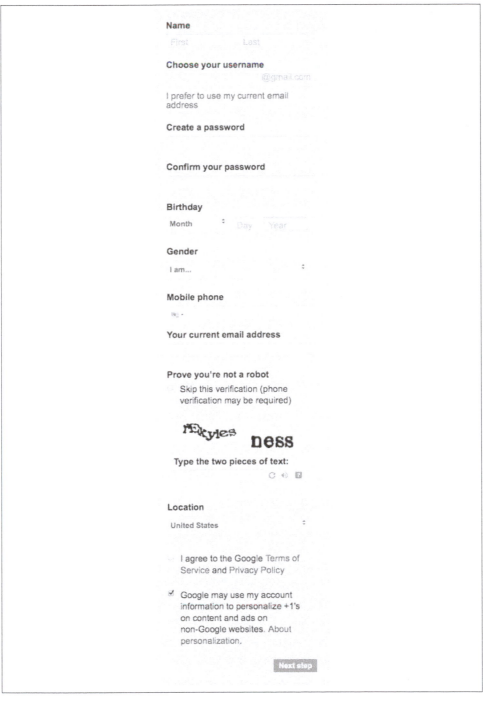

Figure 8-2. Sign up for Google Play

Once you have signed in or signed up for a Google account, you will be asked to accept the Google Play Developer distribution agreement, as shown in Figure 8-3.

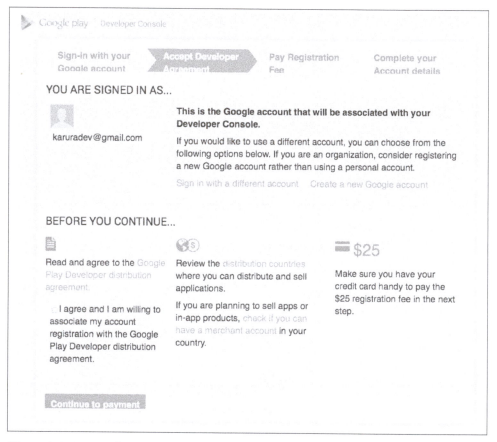

Figure 8-3. Accept the Google Play Developer distribution agreement

Here's a summary of terms of agreement:

- You are a developer in good standing and you will follow the process as described in the agreement for publishing applications on Google Play.
- For paid applications, the payments will be processed using a valid payment processor like Google Checkout.
- For paid applications, a transaction fees of 30% (at the moment) is applied on each application, subscription, or in-app purchase.
- You are responsible for remitting the appropriate taxes to tax authorities.

- You cannot redirect the application to a server that charges fees for the application without using a Google approved payment processor. You can do so if your application does not direct users to the website.

- Refunds for applications are allowed within 15 minutes of application purchase. Refunds are not available to users who have previewed the product before purchase.

- As an application developer, you are expected to provide appropriate post-purchase support to users, if such support is not provided, then the Google can refund the amount that was charged for the application.

- As a developer, you are expected to protect the privacy and legal rights of the user.

- Google will continue to maintain the rating of your application using past historical data and user feedback for your application, which can be displayed to users without prior permission.

- You are also providing a "non-exclusive, worldwide, perpetual license to perform, display and use the product on any device."

Google charges a nominal fees as part of setting up the developer account. Among other things, this is used to establish a valid payer identity. Currently, Google charges a one time $25 fee for this purpose. Upon acceptance of the Google Play Developer Distribution Agreement (GPDDA), you will be redirected to the Google Wallet setup page where you can provide payment details for the developer account fees. As you complete the payment process, you will be redirected to the Developer Console.

Developer Console

Developer Console is the developer's landing page for distributing apps on Google Play. From the Developer Console, you can set up a merchant account in Google Checkout (so you can charge for your applications), upload applications, and get information about your uploaded applications, among other things. You will be redirected to the Developer Console once you have successfully signed up for a developer account.

A merchant account is required if you plan to charge users for your apps. You can set up a merchant account easily by clicking on the Google Merchant Account link, and then filling out a merchant account setup form. Setting up a merchant account is an optional task, but if you do not set one up, you will not be able to charge users for apps, subscriptions, and in-app purchases.

The Developer Console will also allow you to:

- Review and download application analytics for distribution across various android versions, languages, and devices including user churn
- Upload, update, and republish applications

- Access application crash logs and application freezes (including full-stack trace for the thread that crashed)

- View and respond to user comments

- View application ratings

- Manage editorial and marketing material for your apps, to be displayed on potentially multimodal store fronts as in marketing material for web- and device-based Google Play applications.

 You will need to provide a US Federal Tax ID (EIN), a credit card number, and a US Social Security Number (SSN) to set up a merchant account. This information is used to validate your financial information.

Uploading an Application

Once you have created your developer account, you can upload your application on Google Play. The following section will guide you through the necessary steps.

1. On the Developer Console, click on the Add New Application button, shown in Figure 8-4.

Figure 8-4. Add New Application button

2. This will launch a pop-up window where you can specify the title of your application and begin the application upload process, as shown in Figure 8-5.

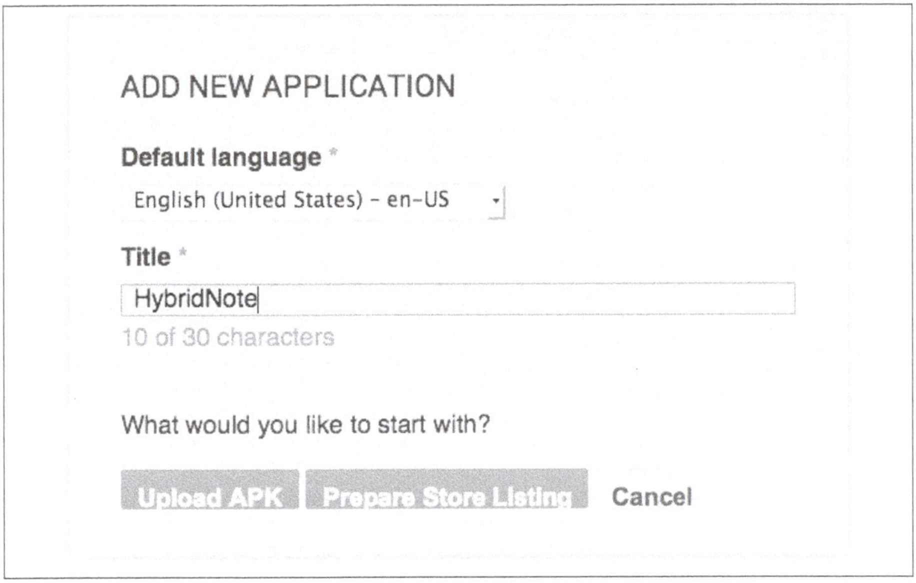

ADD NEW APPLICATION

Default language *

English (United States) – en–US   ▾

Title *

HybridNote

10 of 30 characters

What would you like to start with?

Upload APK | Prepare Store Listing   Cancel

Figure 8-5. Specify the application title

3. Once you have specified the application title, you can either upload the APK for the application or if the APK is not available, you can start working on the store listing. You can do either one in any order, and do not worry, this pop up is just for convenience. You can always go back to your Developer Console and upload a new APK or modify the marketing information before or after publishing the application. Go ahead and click the Prepare Market Listing button. This will open a new form wherein you can enter more detailed marketing information about your application as shown in Figure 8-6.

Figure 8-6. Prepare Market Listing

You can complete this form and save drafts of works in progress as well.

4. Upload the APK.

    Starting May 2013, Google Play allows developers to manage alpha and beta programs for their applications. As a result, the application upload process has been slightly modified. Now as part of the APK tab on the Google Play, you will see three options, one each for Production, Alpha, and Beta programs. For alpha and beta distributions, you can define a Google+ Circle of users who will be part of these distribution channels. Once your Circle has been defined, you can upload and share your application with alpha and beta testers.

    Once you are satisfied with the alpha and beta testing of your application, you can upload the application on the production channel for it to be published, as shown in Figure 8-7.

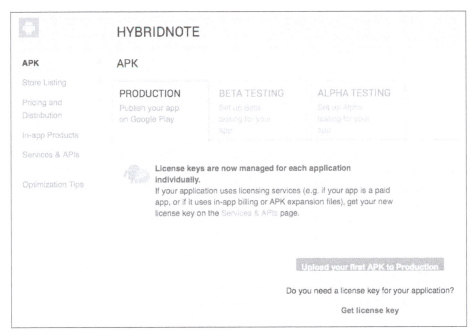

Figure 8-7. *Uploading the application*

5. Set the pricing model.

    After uploading the APK for production, you will have to select the pricing model for your application. In simple terms, you will specify whether you would like to charge for the application and how much would you like to charge for it. You will also select the countries in which you would like to distribute your application. See Figure 8-8.

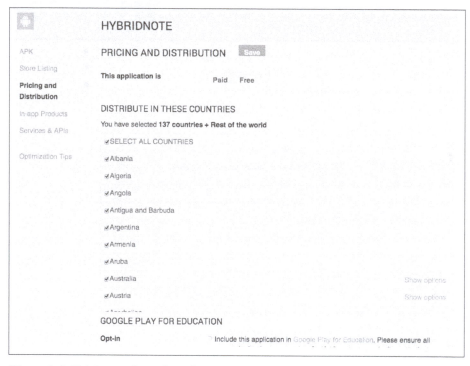

Figure 8-8. Pricing and market selection

Once you have entered all the required details for your application, you will see a Publish Now button, which will allow you to publish the application on Google Play. The application should become immediately available (as in Figure 8-9), however in some instances, we have seen that it can take anywhere between 10—30 minutes before an application shows up in Google Play apps.

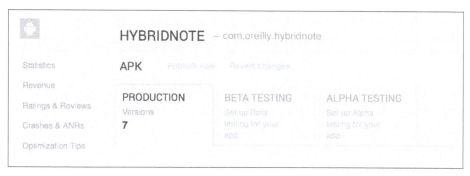

Figure 8-9. Published application on Google Play

Amazon App Store

To publish an Android application on the Amazon App Store, follow these steps:

1. Create a release build for the application.
2. Once the application has been thoroughly tested, digitally sign the application.
3. Publish the application.

In addition to the release activities set forth earlier in this chapter, you may want to:

1. Make sure the Manifest file uses the tag for supporting large screens, which is `<supports-screen android:largeScreens="true"/>`.
2. Remove any dependence on Google-specific APIs and libraries not available on Amazon devices. The most important being license verification library, maps, and in-app billing.
3. Confirm that the application does not require any features not available on Kindle Fire devices.

To publish Android applications on Amazon App Store, you need to join the Amazon App Store Developer Program. The only way to publish applications for Kindle Fire is through the Amazon App Store, so this is a requirement for developing for this device. To sign up, you need a valid Amazon account. Then, go to the Amazon App Store Developer Program website (*https://developer.amazon.com/welcome.html*), click the Create an Account button, and fill in the relevant information for your developer account. The Amazon App Store Developer Program has a fee of $99 a year, which has currently been waived for the first year.

As part of the signup process, you are asked to provide information such as your name, address, phone number, and company information. You then need to review and accept the Developer License Agreement. Read the Developer License Agreement carefully. It is nonexclusive, but it is more restrictive than other publishing options, such as the Android Market. For example, you are required to provide technical and product support to end users and respond to support requests from the Amazon App Store team in a timely fashion.

Self-Signing and the Amazon App Store

The Amazon App Store prefers that you use a certificate provided by Amazon that is tied to your Amazon developer account. In some cases, Amazon even allows users to publish self-signed apps, however, you may have to contact Amazon for those privileges. Either way, once you have the certificate with which you wish to sign the app, you can sign the application using the procedure described earlier in this chapter.

Amazon App Store Sign Up Process

Amazon developer registration beings with signing into your Amazon account, as shown in Figure 8-10. Although, you can also use your existing Amazon account, it is always a good practice to set up a new account for this purpose in the long run.

Figure 8-10. Sign into an Amazon account

On the sign-up screen (shown in Figure 8-11) you will be asked to select your Amazon username, email address, and password.

Figure 8-11. The sign-up screen

Once you successfully sign up and sign in with an Amazon account, you will be redirected to the developer registration page, as shown in Figure 8-12. Here you are required to fill in your contact details, which can then be used by Amazon for publishing purposes.

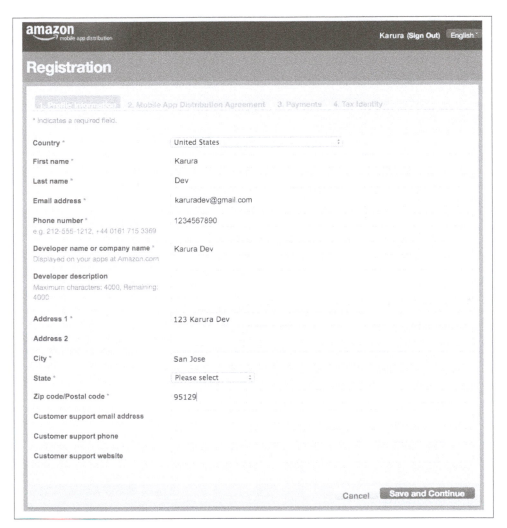

Figure 8-12. Filling in your contact details

 Not all details will be shown to the users. Some of these contact details are used for customer support and for Amazon to reach out to developers in case of a need or urgency.

Once you have provided the contact information, you will be redirected to the Mobile Application Distribution Agreement, shown in Figure 8-13, which you must accept to publish applications through this channel. Please go through the agreement, if you agree with the terms, accept the agreement to move onto the next phase of registration.

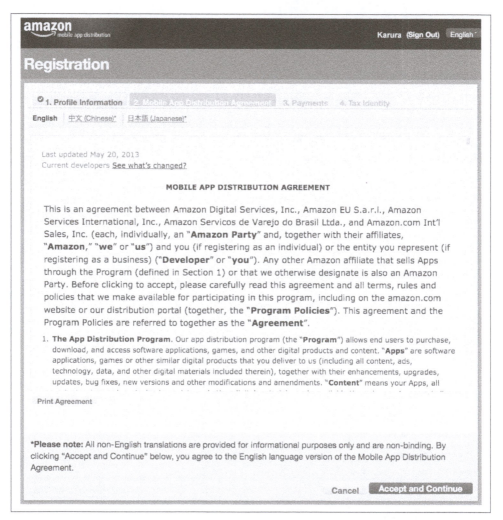

Figure 8-13. Amazon Mobile App Distribution Agreement

On the Payments screen, shown in Figure 8-14, you can specify whether you would like to charge for your applications on the Amazon App Store. Based on your answer, you may have to fill in the Tax Identity questionnaire shown in Figure 8-15. You can change this option later on at any time.

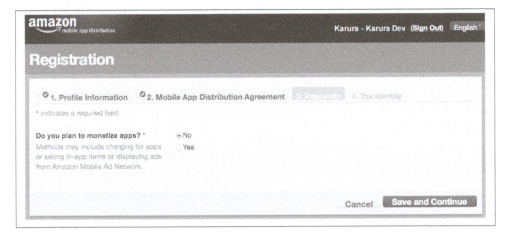

Figure 8-14. Payment profile

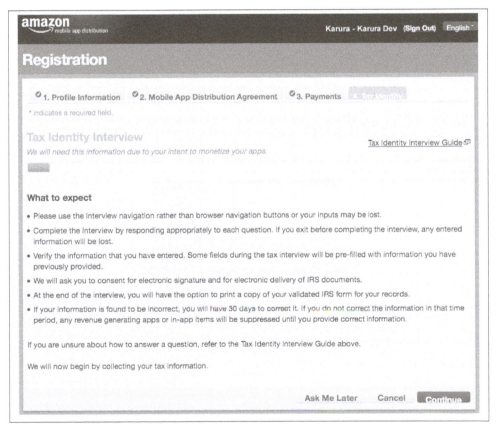

Figure 8-15. Tax Identity questionnaire

As in the case of Google Play, Amazon requires your tax-related information to furnish payments related to application sales. You may choose to fill this form later by selecting the Ask Me Later option. Please note that this information has to be provided before you can publish your applications that are subject to monetization.

At this stage, you can now upload your application packages for review and eventual publication. Figure 8-16 shows the Developer Dashboard.

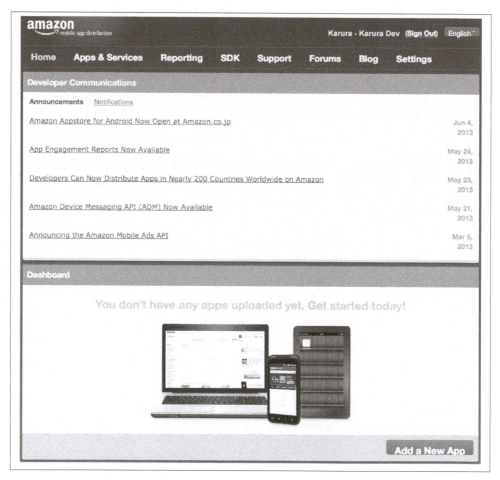

Figure 8-16. Developer Dashboard

Uploading an Application

Uploading the application to the Amazon App Store is quite straightforward, and is similar in principle to the process you will follow on Google Play. Through the help of following figure, we are capturing at a very high level the process involved in uploading and publishing an application through Amazon App Store.

To upload a new application, tap on the Add a New App button in the My Apps section, shown in Figure 8-17. This will initiate the application submission workflow, wherein you can provide general information, pricing, and marketing material for the application.

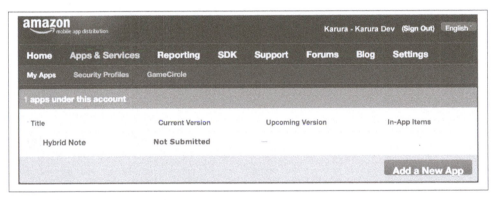

Figure 8-17. Add a new application

The first form to be displayed as part of the workflow is the General Description form (see Figure 8-18). On this form you will enter the public name of the application, your personal tracking number, the category of app, and customer support information, among other things.

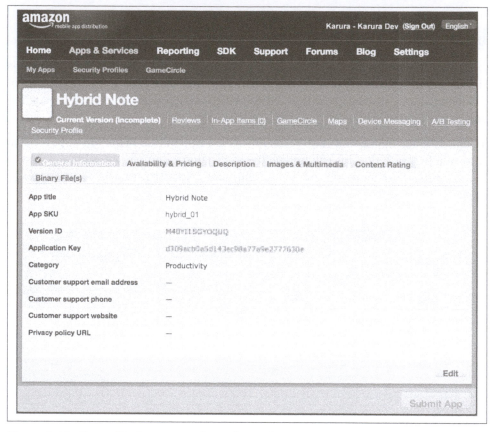

Figure 8-18. General information about the application

After you complete the General Description form, you will be taken to the Availability and Pricing page where you can select the markets and pricing model for your application; see Figure 8-19. You can change this information any time, even after publishing the application. However, please note that even if you change the price plans, users who have downloaded your application will retain access to updates without paying for them.

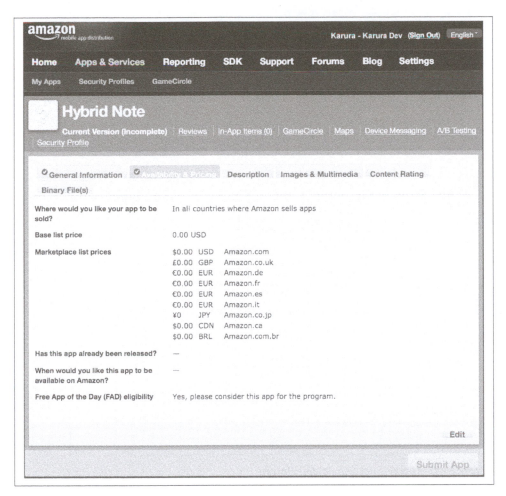

Figure 8-19. Availability and Pricing

On the next page, you will be asked to enter some marketing text describing your application; see Figure 8-20. Note that on this page, you can add multiple translations of the marketing text. If you wish to distribute your application in multiple geographies then, it is important that you publish your marketing content in multiple languages as to allow users to discover apps in their native language. In our experience, this greatly enhances the application uptake.

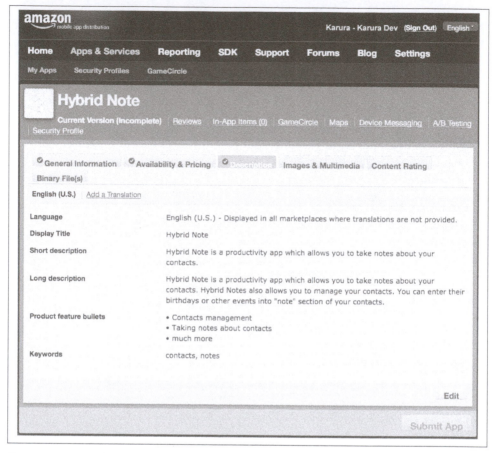

Figure 8-20. Marketing content description

A single picture is equivalent to a thousand words, and this phrase holds equally well for your marketing material. The Amazon App Store allows developers to add screenshots of their application to be displayed to the users before the purchase, as shown in Figure 8-21. As in the case of text, it is always a good practice to make sure that you upload the key screenshots of your app. You may also localize these screenshots to ensure that users can see the application in their native language. Because users often make the decision to purchase an app by relying on what they see as opposed to what they read, you are advised to give special attention to this form.

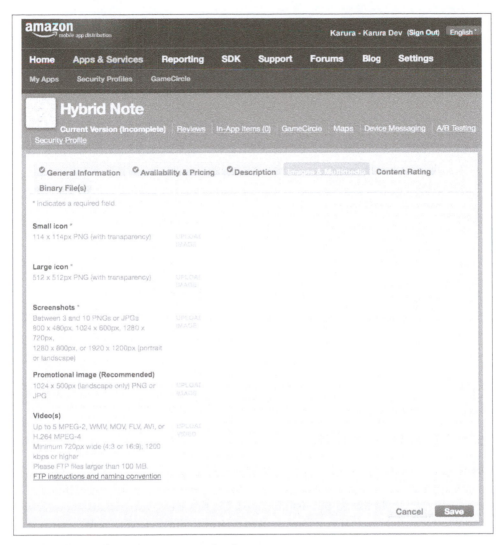

Figure 8-21. Multimedia content upload

Content ratings are an important part of application meta data. They allow the App Store to filter content based on user profiles. As part of each application upload process, you are expected to provide suggested content ratings for your application; see Figure 8-22. It is important to note, that as part of the application review process, Amazon will ensure that your application does not violate the content guidelines and that it matches the content rating entered by you. If the application is found to violate the content rating, then they can reject the application from being published.

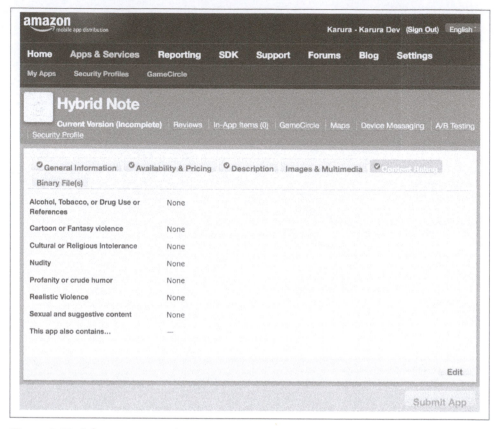

Figure 8-22. Select content rating

The final step of the application submission process is to upload the Android package for you application, as shown in Figure 8-23. On this page, you can also select the devices for which you would like to publish the apps. On this page, you can also specify any special test instructions that you may want to pass onto the reviewers at Amazon. Once you have uploaded the binary and filled in the correct information, the Submit App button at the bottom of the page will be enabled. The application can be then submitted for review by clicking on this button.

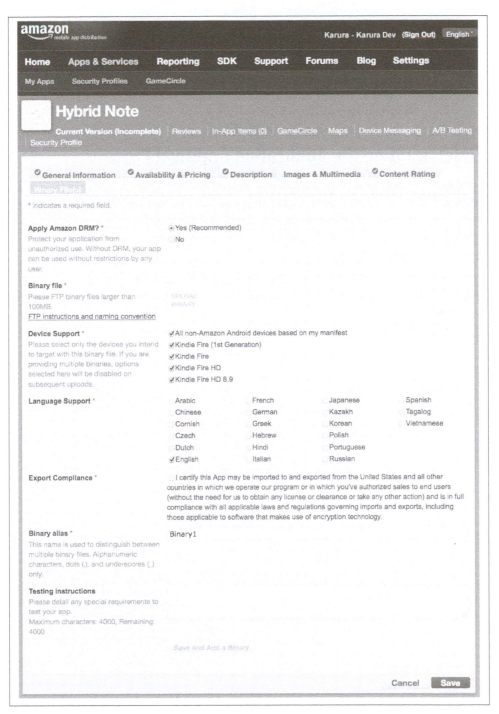

Figure 8-23. Upload the application package

If the application is rejected during the review process, you will be given instructions describing the reasons for rejection. Once you have taken care of the Amazon content guidelines, you can resubmit the application using the process described earlier except that instead of creating a new application, you will modify and submit the existing one from your dashboard.

Understanding the Application Approval Process

Upon submission, the application will be reviewed and tested by the Amazon App Store developer team to ensure that it follows the guidelines set forth in the developer agreement. Once reviewed, it will either be Approved, Rejected, or Pending. For Pending and Rejected statuses, you will receive an email with an explanation.

After your application successfully makes it through the review process, it is published. Once it's published, the status of the application changes to Live. If at some point in the future the application is removed from the Amazon App Store, its status is marked as Suppressed.

About the Authors

Nizamettin Gok (aka Nizam) has more than 15 years of experience in client-side applications. He has been involved in designing, developing, and managing large-scale web applications for many years. He has since translated his experiences into working in the mobile application space during his time in Japan.

Nizam believes that the invention of Ajax technology was a turning point for client-side applications. His focus on using JavaScript in mobile web applications led him to building hybrid applications for Android. He is very passionate about creating excellent user experiences.

He has a personal interest in web application security; in his free time he currently maintains Geoxies (*http://www.geoxies.com*) (a site that helps prevent fraudulent activities). Nizam has also managed small- to large-scale and offshore teams successfully. He is currently working at Microsoft as a Senior Software Development Engineer for the Skype Android platform.

Nitin Khanna is a lead engineer for Android at Skype with extensive experience in mobile application development for Android, iOS, Symbian, and BREW. In his free time, Nitin contributes to many open source projects. He also has experience in OS middleware and protocol stack development.

Colophon

The animal on the cover of *Building Hybrid Android Apps with Java and JavaScript* is a pacuma toadfish (*Batrachoides surinamensis*). This species of toadfish can be found in the Caribbean Sea and the Atlantic Ocean, with habitats stretching along the coast of Central and South America from Honduras to Brazil. The pacuma toadfish is the largest species of toadfish, reaching up to 22 inches in length. They generally stay fairly inactive, disguising themselves in the sand or mud of shallow warm water.

Despite being harvested as a commercial food source and inhabiting environments that undergo large-scale fluctuations, this species has proven tolerant and resilient to changing environment conditions, spawning from 400 to 500 eggs at a time.

The cover image is from a loose plate, source unknown. The cover font is Adobe ITC Garamond. The text font is Adobe Minion Pro; the heading font is Adobe Myriad Condensed; and the code font is Dalton Maag's Ubuntu Mono.

Have it your way.

Get even more for your money.

Join the O'Reilly Community, and register the O'Reilly books you own. It's free, and you'll get:

- $4.99 ebook upgrade offer
- 40% upgrade offer on O'Reilly print books
- Membership discounts on books and events
- Free lifetime updates to ebooks and videos
- Multiple ebook formats, DRM FREE
- Participation in the O'Reilly community
- Newsletters
- Account management
- 100% Satisfaction Guarantee

Signing up is easy:

1. Go to: oreilly.com/go/register
2. Create an O'Reilly login.
3. Provide your address.
4. Register your books.

Note: English-language books only

To order books online:
oreilly.com/store

For questions about products or an order:
orders@oreilly.com

To sign up to get topic-specific email announcements and/or news about upcoming books, conferences, special offers, and new technologies:
elists@oreilly.com

For technical questions about book content:
booktech@oreilly.com

To submit new book proposals to our editors:
proposals@oreilly.com

O'Reilly books are available in multiple DRM-free ebook formats. For more information:
oreilly.com/ebooks

O'REILLY®

Spreading the knowledge of innovators   oreilly.com